CHECK YOUR CHARACTER

Putting the Beatitudes Into Practice

by Knofel Staton

Cover Photo
© 1980, Robert C. Hayes

New Life BOOKS

A division of STANDARD PUBLISHING
Cincinnati, Ohio
39992

Staton, Knofel

  Check your character.

  1. Beatitudes. 2. Christian life—1960-
I. Title.
BT382.S754   248.4   80-19950
ISBN 0-87239-421-2

Instructor's Guide

Are you ready to do some soul-searching? Are you ready to look deeply into your inner being? Are you ready to evaluate your inner motivations, your deepest thoughts, your basic attitudes? Are you ready to compare your character with the character that God intends for you to have? Are you ready to patch up the cracks in your character? Are you determined to have your character and behavior molded after Christ's example?

The Guide

As the teacher, you must seriously seek to answer these questions in the affirmative and then commit yourself to lead your students on their individual soul-searching expeditions. Being the guide for the journey, you must prepare yourself by reading the textbook in its entirety, by taking the "Check Your Character" tests yourself (at the end of each chapter), and by deciding on the main thrust of the book and the emphasis of each chapter.

Study each chapter separately, reading the Scripture references carefully—getting a real "handle" on each quality discussed. Make note of the practical applications that would be particularly relevant to your students, and then be ready to lead the class in a discussion of them.

Finally, bolster all your preparations with much prayer. Helping students delve deeply within themselves necessitates the guidance of the Holy Spirit.

The Motivation

To gain the most benefit from an expedition through the truths of the Scripture emphasized in this book, your student must *want* to go on the journey; they must *want* to engage in the search of their souls. The aspects of character discussed are intensely personal, and the study will not be successful unless each individual becomes truly concerned about his inner motivations and thoughts.

You will know best how to motivate your students to embark on this personal expedition, but here are a few suggestions:

(1) Ask your class the following questions (either orally or written). Allow them time to think about them individually or give them time to write down their thoughts (but don't make it a sharing time):

a. Do you consider yourself a happy person?
b. Do you consider yourself a satisfied and "at peace" person?
c. Are you happy with your family life?
d. Are you happy with your career?
e. Are you happy with your friends?
f. Are you happy with your church work and relationships?
g. Are you happy with yourself? With the way you look? With the way you act? With the way you are on the inside?
h. Do you feel ashamed or frightened by the thought that God looks deeply into your inner being, knowing your every thought and motivation?

(2) Review briefly for the class the life of Job,

emphasizing his many problems and relating them to current parallels: economic deprivation (loss of possessions and wealth), loss of health (continuous discomfort and pain), loss of family (death of all children and their families), spiritual onslaught (attack of the devil), loss of friends' support.

Then ask your class: If all these problems befell you, could you handle it? Would you be able to cope? Could you remain a true-blue Christian? A sterling example to all around you? Or would you crumble? Would you drown in your troubles and pain?

(3) Have on display a large mirror. Have each student pass in front of the mirror and look at themselves for five-ten seconds (with large class choose a few for the demonstration). How many will be able to look at themselves "straight in the eye" for that period of time without giggling or being embarrassed? Discuss why such an exercise was difficult. Then ask them these questions:

a. If you were asked to look into the mirror of your soul—your inner being, your inner thoughts, your true, real feelings and motivations—could you do so without shame, fear, or embarrassment?

b. Or would you try to look away from and ignore what you know is there?

The Goal

Now that your students feel the need to look more deeply into their inner beings, and are curious about where a soul search will lead them, make clear to them what results this expedition will reap for them personally:

A. They will discover what true happiness is and how they can achieve it.

B. They will see the picture of the character—the soul, the inner being—that God expects us to be.

C. They will discover how they can live victoriously no matter what problems and troubles come their way.

Write these goals on the chalkboard or on poster board, so they can be visible throughout the lessons. At the end of each chapter, have the class point out how the study emphasized one or all of these goals.

The Gear

Every expedition needs the proper equipment. Encourage each student to study the Scripture references and the text of each chapter before coming to class. Stress the importance of each student having an open mind and the willingness to delve deeply into his/her own character and personality.

The Signposts

Visuals would be very important aids in these studies. A distinct quality is considered in each chapter, and each quality builds upon the one before it. All the qualities linked together are needed to fill out the strong, buoyant character that God wishes us to have. A well-utilized visual would impress this upon the students and could also help in reviewing.

Here are some suggestions: (1) each quality pictured as a link in a chain (add a link for each chapter, making the chain stronger with each addition which is anchored to the goals of happiness and buoyancy; (2) each quality pictured as a step on a staircase (label each step as each quality is considered, having the goals at the top); (3) have an outline of a person's body (placing each quality on the outline during each chapter study), with the goal being a mature Christian character.

The Plan

In the opening of each chapter, spend around five minutes getting the class's attention and sparking their interest in the quality under consideration. Then through lecture and a group study of the Scripture references, make the meaning of the quality (as Jesus meant it to be) clear. Real life illustrations as well as other Scriptural examples would be helpful. Have the class discuss two or three thought questions to make certain the quality is understood fully.

Allow plenty of time for the class to think about and discuss the practical applications.

For the last eight-ten minutes of the class period, give your students time to evaluate themselves by filling out the "Check Your Character" test at the end of the chapter. This should not be a sharing time, but a time for personal introspection and commitment. Encourage them to pray, to meditate, and to make definite plans to incorporate the truths they have learned into their lives.

Chapter One
Main Emphasis—Being a Buoyant Christian
Main Points:
    I. It's What Is on the Inside That Counts
    II. Becoming a Child of God
    III. Achieving Christlike Qualities
Thoughtful Questions:
    1. Besides the buoy, what other examples can you give about the importance of the insides?
    2. Why should every Christian have an optimistic outlook on life?
    3. Why can't non-Christians have truly buoyant lives?
    4. List some ways we can show that we are proud to be seeking to be God's clones.
    5. What problems put you in a tailspin the fastest?
Practical Application:
    1. Discuss: A Christian family has just lost all of their earthly possessions in a fire. What would you *say* and *do* to encourage them to remain afloat during the storm?
    2. Give examples from your own experiences about how you remained victorious when the times were dark.
    3. Look at your own character. List your strengths and weaknesses. Keep your list, refer to it, and change it as you study each chapter.

Chapter Two
Main Emphasis—Humility
Main Points:
    I. Man's Need
    II. The Cry for Help

III. Meaning of Humility

IV. The Reward

Thought Questions:

1. What other reasons can you give why our prosperity makes Christianity difficult?

2. Why do you feel the attitude of dependence on others is so repugnant to the average American?

3. Give example of how people today cry out to God for help but cannot accept His solution.

4. What are God's provisions for our salvation?

5. Why do we need our fellow Christians?

6. What should be the Christian's attitude toward his possessions?

Practical Application:

1. Study Acts 2:44-47; 4:32-37; 5:1-10. Find the illustrations in these passages of the quality "poor in spirit." Discuss how Ananias and Sapphira displayed their lack of this quality. Consider how these principles can be applied in church life today.

2. Discuss ways to encourage the interdependence between the members of your congregation.

3. Summarize by listing the thoughts that a "poor in spirit" person must have. Look for them in the chapter and verbalize them.

Chapter Three
Main Emphasis—Godly Sorrow
Main Points:

I. Meaning of Mourning

II. Mourning Over Sin

III. The Comfort

Thought Questions:

1. Contrast God's type of sorrow with the sorrow we usually see in the world.

2. How does our involvement in the church sharpen our consciences?

3. Read 1 Corinthians 5. What had resulted because of the lack of mourning? What was Paul's suggestion for a solution?

4. List all the reasons why we should be concerned for the lost.

Practical Applications:

1. A Christian man in your Bible school is blatantly sinning. Discuss what steps should be taken by the class to seek to rescue him from Satan. Read Galatians 6:1; James 5:19, 20; 1 Corinthians 5.

2. Devise a plan for your class' outreach to the lost of your community during the next month. Then put it into effect.

3. Have the class list the most prevalent sins in your community, and then decide what your class should do about them.

Chapter Four
Main Emphasis—Let God Have Control

Main Points:

  I. Common Reactions to Problems
 II. The Power of Gentleness
III. Controlled Reactions
 IV. The Reward

Thought Questions:

1. Give examples of persons' reactions to failure by withdrawing or retaliating.

2. How does the philosophy of Dr. Wayne W. Dyer *(Your Erroneous Zones* and *Pulling Your Own Strings)* differ from how a Christian should think?

3. Should a "meek" person ever assert himself?

4. Discuss the similarities between "meekness" and the quality of "poor in spirit" from Chapter 2. Decide how the two qualities are distinct but related.

Practical Application:

1. Study the following Scriptures, decide how they illustrate meekness, and apply the principles to life today: Ephesians 4:31, 32; Matthew 5:39; 7:1; 1 Corinthians 6:1-7; 2 Timothy 2:25; James 1:21.

2. Discuss how a "meek" person would handle the following situations:

a. An irate neighbor complains about your son practicing on his drums.

b. You bought a TV recently. It never has worked right, and the store keeps giving you the runaround.

c. You are in college and you share an apartment with two other persons. Your roommates have to be reminded over and over again to pick up after themselves. You come home to find the house in complete chaos.

d. Your boss seems to "have it in for you."

Chapter Five
Main Emphasis—Constant Craving for Good
Main Points:
    I. Feeling Hunger

II. Bearing the Fruit

III. Sharpening the Appetite

Thought Questions:

1. Where do we find God's menu, and what steps must we take in order to partake of it?

2. What are the dangers in becoming satisfied with our spirituality?

3. Why does God feel we have the responsibility to feed others?

4. What effects can Satan and his devices have upon our spiritual appetites?

Practical Application:

1. Have each student devise his own plan for feeding himself spiritually. Write it down in specific detail—what he will do, when, for how long, etc.

2. Have the students discuss together how they will improve in their efforts to feed others spiritually. Devise and write down a plan.

Chapter Six

Main Emphasis—Satisfaction of Righteousness

Main Points:

I. Definition of Righteousness

II. How to Become Righteous

III. Being Satisfied

Thought Questions:

1. Why is our relationship with God dependent on our relationships with others, and vice versa?

2. If the law was not to make us righteous, then why have it?

3. Why can't a non-Christian be truly righteous?

4. Will we be able to tell when another person is righteous? Will we be able to tell when one is pretending to be righteous?

Practical Application:

Have each student write a composition describing how his inner life and his outer conduct coincide as his defense before God on Judgment Day. (This should be an individual activity, not shared.)

Chapter Seven
Main Emphasis—All the Aspects of Mercy

Main Thoughts:

    I. Definition of Mercy

   II. How to Show Mercy

Thought Questions:

1. Why can we say that God is the perfect example of mercy?

2. Is your congregation's mercy as extensive as Christ's? Give proof.

3. Why is it not possible to be isolationists and evangelists at the same time?

4. How has your congregation allowed the "machinery" to supersede the personal acts of mercy?

Practical Application:

1. Share how someone's mercy to you changed your life.

2. Have each student determine how he is going to improve his showing of mercy. Ask him to write down definite plans.

3. Study John 5:4-8, noting verse 6. Then discuss whether desiring to receive mercy should be a prerequisite.

4. Discuss how a person should receive mercy. Read Luke 17:11-14 and Romans 15:9.

Chapter Eight
Main Emphasis—Inner Purity
Main Points:

I. Meaning of Heart
II. Meaning of Purity
III. Importance of Pure Motives
IV. How to Remain Pure in Heart

Thought Questions:

1. Does our remaining steadfast in the faith always mean we have pure motivations?

2. How is inner purity a type of freedom?

3. What does it mean to be double-minded?

4. What is the importance of a right goal?

5. How can a person be nontraditional and be right? And be wrong?

6. What are the dangers involved in judging by outward appearances?

Practical Application:

Discuss what the proper motivation would be, and what a motivation of pretense or selfishness would be, in the following aspects of behavior:

a. attending a church service
b. singing in the church choir
c. helping a poor family
d. complimenting your wife/husband—boyfriend/girlfriend
e. fulfilling your responsibility on the job
f. volunteering to be on a church committee
g. contributing to the church offering
h. calling on a neighbor

Chapter Nine
Main Emphasis—Spiritual Peace
Main Points:

I. The Peace Within

II. Making Peace

III. Maintaining Peace

Thought Questions:

1. Discuss the differences between God's view of peace and the world's view.

2. When was peace lost for mankind, and when was it restored?

3. Why is it necessary to have turmoil or tribulation before you know whether you have peace or not?

4. Describe a peacemaker's attitude.

5. How can you have a proper self-image and also be a peacemaker?

Practical Application:

How would a peacemaker handle the following situations?

a. Husband and wife disagree about how to handle their rebellious teenager.

b. The leader of the church choir and the minister do not agree about what musical program to present for Christmas.

c. A person in the Sunday-school class is constantly criticizing the teacher and is always negative about the class projects.

d. There is a feud in the office; the coworkers want you to take sides.

e. A group of youth are consistently tearing up the church bus.

f. Vicious gossip about your best friend is spreading through the community.

Chapter Ten
Main Emphasis—Handling Persecution
Main Points:
   I. Types and Causes of Persecution
   II. Reaction to Persecution
Thought Questions:
   1. What are the main causes of persecution?
   2. How can the church be *in* the world but not *of* the world?
   3. When the Jews were persecuted by the Germans, did they react properly?
   4. Why is the principle expressed in Romans 12:19-21 so hard to swallow?
   5. In what ways do we invite persecution?
   6. What might be the problem if there is no one persecuting you?
Practical Application:
   1. Study John 17. How do the principles expressed relate to our study in this chapter? How can we apply these principles in our church today? Be specific.
   2. Formulate a plan of how to evangelize a non-Christian who is constantly badgering the church and its program.
   3. If Madalyn M. O'Hair (avowed atheist) came to your town and wanted to have a public debate with a Christian, what should be done?
                              —Prepared by Julia Staton

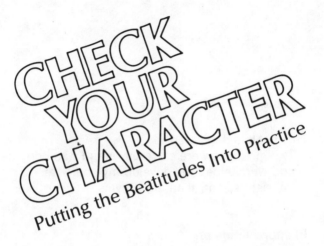

CHECK YOUR CHARACTER

Putting the Beatitudes Into Practice

by Knofel Staton

Cover Photo
© 1980, Robert C. Hayes

A division of STANDARD PUBLISHING
Cincinnati, Ohio
39993

This book is dedicated to:
    Two girls who were close by when I was born
    and who helped me develop my character—
    my sisters, Ima Jean and Phyllis.

In appreciation of:
    my wife, Julia, who typed and edited the
    first draft from my handwritten scribbling,
    and to Mrs. Nancy Presko who typed the
    final manuscript.

ISBN: 0-87239-422-0

Copyright © 1981. The STANDARD PUBLISHING Company, Cincinnati, Ohio.
Division of STANDEX INTERNATIONAL Corporation.
Printed in U.S.A.

Preface

The Beatitudes in the Sermon on the Mount have been referred to as the "beautiful attitudes" of Jesus. They are indeed that, for as we look into their meaning and application we are looking into the very being of Jesus himself.

Behind every activity of Jesus which is recorded for us in the Gospels, we can discover one of these beautiful attitudes. Rightly so, because attitudes result in actions. They are not just about the "inside" of a person, but they also affect the "outside" of a person.

In speaking about these attitudes, Jesus is saying to each of us, "Look at yourself. Look at what you were meant to be. Are you living up to your potential?" It is as if we were standing naked in front of a mirror. Our every thought and action is exposed.

In seeking to discover the meaning of these Beatitudes, I researched every place the words of each Beatitude were used in the Old and New Testaments. That turned out to be a rich experience for me. Now I'm seeking to share with you the meaning of the Beatitudes as well as the application for our lives today.

Study this book with your own lifestyle and character in mind. Keep asking yourself, "Is my character matching up favorably to what God expects?" Then have the courage to admit your failures and gain the strength and motivation to allow Christ to make the changes in you.

You matter to God. Your mind matters to God. Your heart matters to God. Your attitudes matter to God. Your behavior matters to God. May your being become *whole* as you seek to imitate the Master and the Father.

All Scripture quotations are from the New American Standard Bible, unless otherwise indicated.

—*Knofel Staton*

Contents

Chapter 1

"Blessed Are You . . ."

Where in the world could it possibly be? With exasperation seeping out of every pore, I started the rounds again. Where could that watch be? I retraced all my steps. The bedroom? No. The kitchen? No. Maybe the end table in the living room. Not there either. The bathroom? I pictured every part of the bathroom in my mind, for I had already been in there three times looking for the watch. The tub? No. The vanity? No. The clothes hamper? No. The toilet? The toilet! Oh, no! To the bathroom I ran.

There it was lying peacefully in the bottom of the toilet bowl. And just as I was elbow deep, seeking to retrieve the watch, in walked our sixteen-month-old son. "Watch. . .DaDa?" he queried.

My wife was in the hospital with our one-day-old daughter; and I was in charge of our toddler at home. I learned so many things in that period. One of them was not to leave my watch alone in the bathroom with a sixteen-month-old boy.

I also learned that a watch will not float and will be damaged if allowed to sink into water. Oh, it was waterproof alright; but I found out what a waterproof watch meant—the repair bill was about one-half the price of a new watch.

Why didn't that watch float? Because it was

made of metal and was too heavy? No, that was not the reason. One can throw a hundred pounds of metal into the water and watch it float. The difference between the watch sinking and a huge metal buoy floating on the water is not the material or the weight, but how it is made and what is on the inside.

A buoy is made of metal and is very heavy, but it floats, for there is air on the inside. Let the winds stir and the waves surge; the buoy will still be floating. The storms may be so fierce that you cannot even see the buoy, but it will still be there. The winds and waves cannot sink it, because a buoy is made to float.

A Buoyed-up Christian

Jesus said many times that a Christian is as a floating buoy. He spotlighted this concept when He began His teaching to the multitudes with the word "blessed."

> Blessed are the poor in spirit . . .
> Blessed are those who mourn . . .
> Blessed are the gentle . . .
> Blessed are those who hunger . . .
> Blessed are the merciful . . .
> Blessed are the pure in heart . . .
> Blessed are the peacemakers . .
> Blessed are those who have been persecuted . . .
> Blessed are you when men revile you. . . .
> —Matthew 5:3-11

The word "blessed" emphasizes that what is on the inside of a person keeps him afloat amidst all the stormy experiences of life. The Christian is made differently from the non-Christian, for he has been remade. He has new material inside him which enables him to "float" no matter what the external circumstances are.

The Christian has *Christ* living within him (Galatians 2:20)—the same Christ who walked on water. The Christian has "divine air" living inside of Him, the very "breath" of God—the *Holy Spirit* (1 Corinthians 6:19). That Spirit of God is eternal and cannot be sunk. The Christian has *God* living within Him (Philippians 2:13). After all the storms blow past, God will be there; He will still be just as powerful and alive as He ever was. The troubled winds and the crashing waves of life do not have the final say. God does! And He lives within the Christian!

The devil is similar to a tornado which seeks to destroy everything in its path. The tornadoes of life assail all of us at one time or another. But even when all else is falling down, the Christian will come surfacing to the top. There will be times when it looks as if the Christian is beaten. But as time passes, the Christian will emerge without a scratch. The apostle Paul said it like this:

> Everything is grinding away at us, but we are not crushed. Life is so distressing, but we are not giving up. We are driven out, but we are not driven down. We are knocked down, but we are not knocked out.
> —2 Corinthians 4:8, 9
> (paraphrase)

How can Christians stay afloat in this way? Paul tells us in the preceding verse: "We have this treasure in earthen vessels" (4:7). The word "vessel" is the Greek word for clay pot. Clay pots were very breakable, but Christians are pots that will not break. Why? Because of what is on the inside: "That the surpassing greatness of the power may be of God and not from ourselves."

Christians can reassure one another that the One who is in us is greater than he who is in the world (1 John 4:4). We can feed each other a steady diet of victory, not defeat.

An unknown poet said it this way:

> One ship drives east and another drives west
> with the very same winds that blow.
> It is the set of the sail and not the gale that
> directs the way they go.

It is the same with us. It is the set of our souls and not the storms that direct the way we go. What lies behind us, around us, or in front of us is tiny and insignificant when compared to Him who lives inside us.

The word "blessed" describes the inner setting of the soul despite the surrounding circumstances. Sometimes the externals seem quite devastating, yet we who are "blessed" live amidst the suffering (James 5:11; 1 Peter 3:14). People may hate us and purposely avoid us (Luke 6:22), people may slander us (1 Peter 4:14), we may face difficult trials (James 1:12) or even death itself (Revelation 14:13), yet through it all we will be called "blessed." Yes, the Christian will stay afloat despite the storm. He will have an inner buoyancy of peace, happiness, radiance, and gladness—blessings that are his because he is in Christ and Christ is in him.

Congratulations!

There is one sight in the Rocky Mountain area of our country that never ceases to amaze me. I will be looking with awe at the mammoth formations of solid rock thousands of feet high, when suddenly I will spot a single, fragile-looking flower breaking through the barren rock formations and actually blooming! When I see that delicate flower fighting against all odds to bloom, I get excited and I yearn to shout, "Congratulations! You've made it!"

The word "blessed" also carries with it the idea of excited congratulations. God is going to give us those congratulations in the future if we die in the Lord (Revelation 14:13), if we stay alert (16:15), if we are a part of the first resurrection (20:6), if we heed His word (22:7), and if our robes have been washed in the blood of the Lamb (7:14).

But His congratulations to us are not reserved for only these future times. He congratulates all those whose inner characters are like His, even when those characters are completely opposite to the character of the world outside. God's congratulations are a present reality.

Jesus was passing out this latter type of congratulations in His Sermon on the Mount. He was congratulating the inner qualities that characterize the children of God. These qualities are from the character of God and were demonstrated by Christ in His own life on earth. Jesus was suggesting that this type of character keeps us afloat during the rough times.

Thus the word "blessed" first of all refers to

God (1 Timothy 1:11; 6:15). He is the eternal buoy because of His kind of character. And that same character can live within us.

The blessings mentioned in the Beatitudes are not simply to be memorized and recited; they are to be realities in our lives. The beginning point for that reality is our uniting with God and receiving forgiveness:

> Blessed are those whose lawless deeds have been forgiven, and whose sins have been covered. Blessed is the man whose sin the Lord will not take into account.
> —Romans 4:7, 8

We have all sinned (Romans 3:23). Our sins are forgiven when we turn our sinful characters over to God through faith and die to that sinful character by repentance. We then buy that sinful character in baptism and rise to walk in a newness of life (Romans 4-6) in which the Spirit of God has taken up residence (Romans 8).

Congratulations to you when your character is united to God's and changed to be like His (1 Peter 4:14). As a Christian each quality of life that Jesus spoke about in the Beatitudes is now living within you. Of course, some of you may be in the infancy stage. That is normal; we all come into the family of God as newborn babes. Then we begin our life of growth. But into what are we growing?

We are growing daily into Christ's image, complete with His characteristics. Paul put it this way:

> To become conformed to the image of His Son.
> —Romans 8:29

> But we all, with unveiled face beholding as in a mirror the glory of the Lord, are being transformed into the same image from glory to glory, just as from the Lord, the Spirit.
> —2 Corinthians 3:18

> Until we all attain to the unity of the faith, and the knowledge of the Son of God, to a mature man, to the measure of the stature which belongs to the fulness of Christ.
> —Ephesians 4:13

> We are to grow up in all aspects into Him, who is the head, even Christ.
> —Ephesians 4:15

We are to live so that people recognize the character of our heavenly Father living within us.

> Let your light shine before men in such a way that they may see your good works, and glorify your Father who is in heaven.
> —Matthew 5:16

God's Clones

Did you know that God is in the "cloning" business? He is seeking to reproduce Himself in you and me. The Beatitudes reveal to us some of the characteristics that God seeks to reproduce in His children.

When I was a young boy, I bought my father a little poem and a picture at the dime store for his birthday. It wasn't much, for I had little money, but he put it in a cheap frame. That was forty years ago, and that poem is still in that same frame and is hanging on the wall in my son's room.

One night after he had gone to bed, I went into his room to copy down the poem because I wanted to use it in a sermon about fathers. He sleepily asked what I was doing. When I told him I was copying down the words of the poem, he said, "You don't have to look at that. I have it memorized. I could tell it to you. It is my favorite poem."

He quoted it:

> When folks tell me I'm like you, Dad,
> I almost burst with pride,
> 'Cause ever since I was a "pup"
> 'standing by your side,
> I've liked the way you faced the world,
> the things you say and do,
> and would be glad to be the chip
> off such a block—as you!

We should want people to see *God in us,* but I'm afraid many of us are too concerned that people see *us.* We should be proud when people see God's characteristics in our lives. We should be seeking to face the world as God does, to say and do as He would want us to, and be glad to be forming the same kind of character that God has. We should realize how privileged and blessed we are to be God's clones.

Now is the time to check your character. Is it too much like *you,* or is it becoming more like Christ every day? If you are developing Christ's characteristics that are revealed in the Beatitudes, then you will be as a buoy in the midst of a stormy sea, you will be as a flower blooming on a rocky cliff, and you will have an inner happiness and joy no matter what the realities of life throw at you. Truly you are to be congratulated!

Chapter 2

Poor Man—Rich Man

"Blessed are the poor in spirit, for theirs is the
kingdom of heaven."
—Matthew 5:3

It is tough to be a Christian in a country like
the United States. It is not tough because the
United States has more immorality than the rest
of the world. Immorality is rather universal. No,
it is not tough because of perversions. But it is
tough to be a Christian amidst our prosperity.

It is tough to have the attitude of a beggar
when you are rich. It is humiliating to ask for
help when you are climbing the ladder of suc-
cess. It is degrading to be someone's servant
when you own an estate yourself. It is discomfit-
ing to wash someone's feet or polish his boots
when you have a house, two cars, a pickup truck,
a camper, a motorcycle, a color television, a
stereo and tape deck, a boat, and a cabin on the
lake.

The Danger of Riches

Jesus said to His disciples once, "Truly I say to
you, it is hard for a rich man to enter the kingdom of heaven" (Matthew 19:23). Jesus was not
saying He disliked or was antagonistic toward
riches. Having cash on earth does not mean an

15

automatic curse from Heaven. No one has ever been or will ever be richer than God. His prosperity makes the earth's richest person look like a pauper.

But riches do have a way of making a person think he can be independent of others. Not long ago a friend of mine said to me, "In five years I am going to be independently rich. That is my goal in life." When I asked why that was his goal, he replied, "I want to be independent from everyone." That is a devastating goal.

When a whole nation of people has that goal, the nation will be divided over everyone's self-interests. The community spirit of the nation will get lost. I've seen this attitude begin in the homes and spread throughout neighborhoods, to the cities and towns, and become like a cancer eating away at our country.

Neighbors used to be real neighbors to each other. We used to borrow a cup of sugar or a bowl of flour. We used to know the families that lived on our block; we used to care if someone in the community was having troubles. We used to help others; we used to feel that we needed each other. But now we have anonymous families who live in anonymous neighborhoods; we have people who rarely care about anyone else but themselves. We have government agencies and town councils that rarely consider what is good for the people when making their decisions.

How did this depersonalization, noninvolvement, and seemingly unfeeling autonomy begin? It began with the distortion of man's attitude toward God and toward himself.

16

The more prosperous we become, the easier it is to have no need for God. If we get sick, we can call a doctor. Who needs God? If we need more things, we can say, "Charge it." Who needs God? If we need food, we can go to the supermarket. Who needs God? If inflation outstrips wages, we can go on strike. Who needs God? If a tornado wipes out our possessions, we can go to the insurance company. Who needs God? If we need more knowledge, we can go to college. Who needs God?

The more prosperous we become, the more we begin to think we don't need anyone else except a few specialists. We feel we certainly don't need the community or the man across the street. No, we can go it alone!

Isn't it interesting that that was the first thing God said was not good? "It is not good for the man to be alone" (Genesis 2:18).

Becoming a Beggar

Jesus emphasized that man should not seek to be independent of others when He uttered the first Beatitude before the multitudes on the mount: "Blessed are the poor in spirit" (Matthew 5:3).

Jesus was talking about a man's perspective and attitude, not about his financial status. He was not saying that the man who is unsuccessful, who lives in lowly surroundings, or who has few things is to be congratulated. Nor was He glorifying laziness or a lack of enthusiasm. He was not telling us to be timid and withdrawn.

Jesus was outlining the initial quality of a child

17

of God. It had to do with one's mental attitude, not one's material assets. A person who is rich in substance could be poor in spirit, and a person who had little in substance could lack such a spirit.

There are three words for "poor" in the Greek New Testament. Two of these words *(penes, penchros)* describe a person who worked for a living but was only able to maintain mere existence. He had the barest of necessities but no extras. In comparison to all others around him, he would be poor.

But the word Jesus used to describe this quality or attitude was a word that had the most impoverished connotations possible *(ptochos)*. He described a person who had absolutely nothing. He was famished and did not have the ability *by himself* to do anything about it. He had reached the bottom of the well and had found it to be dry. And if the well had started flowing again, he would not have a bucket to catch the water.

Such a person would have only one resource. He must ask for help. He must become dependent on others. The root idea of the word Jesus used carried the picture of someone brought to his knees, someone made to crouch *(pte)*. Jesus was describing a beggar—the very opposite of an independent person. The beggar is dependent on others, knows it, and admits it. He has to trust others for his life. He surrenders himself for his own survival. He is like a baby who is at the mercy of someone else.

A child of God is poor in spirit; he realizes that he is spiritually bankrupt. He knows he has no other resource for the survival of his soul other than God. Thus he humbly calls upon God for help. He begs for his salvation. He does not live as if life rotates around him; he lives as if his life rotates around God. He puts God in the center of his life, instead of himself.

The child of God first asks the question. "What shall I do, Lord?" (Acts 22:10; 2:37). And then he does not balk at God's answer because it was not what he had figured out ahead of time it would be.

God has clearly stated that His gift of salvation is given to those who call upon Him and who obey what He tells them to do (John 1:12; Acts 2:38; Galatians 3:26, 27). Forgiveness is offered by Jesus (Hebrews 9:14). And we receive it by our faith (Acts 15:9).

Too many times God's people in the Old Testament argued with God when He answered their cries for help. To do that is to say, "I want your help only on *my* terms. My spirituality does not really rest upon what you say, God. It rests upon what *I* think." People who have this attitude are showing that they have not yet hit rock bottom; they have not yet admitted that God has the only provisions for salvation.

Yes, it is tough to be totally dependent upon another for survival. But unless we do, we will be totally wiped out spiritually. To admit that we are spiritually bankrupt and need God means that we cannot believe that our salvation rests on our church traditions, our family background, our college degrees, our community, our race, our status, or our knowledge. *Paul had all of these*

*things going for him, but he counted it all gar-
bage compared to receiving the greatest and only
gift that saves—Jesus Christ* (Philippians 3:4-8).

Growing as a Beggar

Being poor in spirit does not end with the initial asking for help and receiving of salvation. It
is to be an ongoing attitude of life.

The important military leader who said to
Jesus, "I am not qualified for You to come under
my roof" (Matthew 8:8) was poor in spirit. The
person who prayed simply "God, be merciful to
me, the sinner" (Luke 18:13) was poor in spirit.
The woman who was happy to receive the
crumbs from the table was poor in spirit (Mark
7:28).

Humility

We may begin the Christian life with this attitude but then reach a point when we are all
puffed up with our own "holiness." The more we
mature in knowledge and status, the easier it
becomes to shift from dependence upon God to
depending upon our Bible knowledge or upon
the position we hold in the church. This is one of
the prevalent dangers in getting human recognition for our progress in Christ. The recognition
might come in the package of being elected to a
leadership role in the church, or it might come in
the package of receiving a doctorate in Biblical
studies. Whatever the package, it is so easy to
think, "I've arrived." It is easy to use our position
to force others to do things our way. Diotrephes
was criticized for just such an attitude:

> Diotrephes, who loves to be first among them,
> does not accept what we say. For this reason, if I
> come, I will call attention to his deeds which he
> does, unjustly accusing us with wicked words;
> and not satisfied with this, neither does he him-
> self receive the brethren, and he forbids those
> who desire to do so, and puts them out of the
> church.
>
> —3 John 9, 10

The leader who cannot clean tables at the end of a fellowship meal is not poor in spirit. Jesus wanted people to remember Him as the one who served tables: "But I am among you as the one who serves" (Luke 22:27).

Jesus mingled with the riffraff of His day. He knew that uneducated fishermen could carry on His kind of work. He was ready to drink water from the same cup as a half-breed had drunk. He touched the lepers. He cared about a crazy man.

He spent time in the homes of common people. He took time out of His busy schedule to attend a wedding, go to a party, go fishing with His disciples, notice the children playing, and talk with the beggars that lined the streets. He attended religious services led by others; He was willing to explain answers to questions; He sponsored a picnic; He commended a woman with a bad reputation; He went home with a crook; He paid taxes; He helped a crippled woman who had been ignored by all.

Jesus was the living demonstration of what it means to be poor in spirit. He was humble, and He humbly served.

Jesus had every reason to be puffed up because of who He was. After all, He had been on the throne in Heaven! But He never ceased to make it clear that who He was, what He said, and what He did was of God's making. He never pretended to be a self-made man (John 5:30; 6:38; 12:49).

Interdependence

Growing in Christ with the "poor in spirit" attitude also means we will be dependent and interdependent upon God's people. We first admit our need of God's help, and then we admit our need for the help of other people.

The person who is poor in spirit participates in a submitting-contributing fellowship in Christ's body, the church. The competitive spirit is replaced with the cooperative spirit. Each child of God lives for the family of God as well as for the Father of the family. Each child of God is willing to use his gifts for the well-being of others (Romans 12:10ff; 1 Corinthians 12). He is willing to spot potentialities in others and help them develop those potentialities even though they might become more popular.

One who is poor in spirit considers others to be more important than himself (Philippians 2:3), and he offers himself as a living sacrifice to serve others (2:5-11). He does not use slanderous words because it would hurt others. He lives in submission to others (Ephesians 5:21). He forgives the hurts others direct to him. He lives to maintain the unity of the Spirit in the bond of peace (Ephesians 4:3). He refuses to stir up strife over his opinions.

If he knows a fellow Christian has something

against him, he takes the initiative for reconciliation regardless of whose fault it is (Matthew 5:23, 24). He will seek to make friends with his opponents (5:25), and he can contribute to God's cause without anyone knowing it (6:2-4). He does not go around seeking to find faults in people (7:1-5). He becomes a servant to all (Matthew 20:25-28).

A Poor Man—Rich Man

He was the orphaned son of a slave, a Negro, but he had reached the high status of teaching at a state university. While a professor at Iowa State University, he received a letter from Booker T. Washington, the president of a small struggling college in the south.

Mr. Washington had said, "I cannot offer you money, position or fame. The first two you have; the last you will no doubt receive in the place you now occupy. These things I now ask you to give up. I offer you in their place work—hard, hard work—the task of bringing people from degradation, poverty, and waste to full manhood."

The professor accepted the offer. During his years in that small college in the south, he was often so busy that he forgot to cash his salary checks. He wore the same suit for forty years. In the midst of his great contributions, he was offered what would be the equivalent of millions of dollars on today's market to work for Thomas Edison and Henry Ford. But he refused.

When his friends argued with him, saying he could help his people more if he had the money Edison and Ford would give him, he replied, "If I had all that money, I might forget about my people."

And on his tombstone are carved these words: "He could have added fortune to fame; but caring for neither, he found happiness and honor in being helpful to the world." Yes, George Washington Carver lived out what it means to be poor in spirit.

Becoming Rich

The poor in spirit are to be congratulated, "for theirs is the kingdom of heaven" (Matthew 5:3). The child of God lives under God's kingship. God's will and rule become his will. He is part of God's kingdom, and all that is in that kingdom belongs to him. The poor in spirit are heirs of God's entire kingdom (Romans 8:15-17).

As Christians we are joint owners of all that is God's. We don't have to scheme to acquire it, or sell our souls to gain it. What we do not have an opportunity to enjoy on the earth we can enjoy in Heaven.

Remember the beggar, Lazarus, who was poor in material things as well as poor in spirit? When he died, he was a poor man, rich man. He remained poor in spirit, but he became rich in sustenance (Luke 16:19-31).

Are you poor in spirit? Congratulations! You are joint owner of Wall Street, General Motors, and the Grand Canyon! This world belongs to the King, so the kingdom belongs to His children. Don't be worrying and fretting. Don't be out grabbing all you can get. If you live in the Father's will, you will inherit everything.

24

Check Your Character*

                                                  Yes No

1. Can you admit that you need to be on God's welfare roll?
2. Can you admit that you need other people?
3. Can you name one way that you have been dependent on another Christian this past month?
4. Do you ask God for help daily?
5. Do you ever express to others that you are who you are because of what God does for you?
6. Do you give thanks to God for each meal you eat?
7. Do you thank God for each purchase you are able to make?
8. Do you feel that God owns everything you have?
9. Do you feel putout if you have to do a "dirty" job around the house or around the church?
10. Do you feel you are superior to others?
11. Do you feel little need to study the Scriptures?
12. Do you feel you already know all about the Christian life and doctrines?

*One who is "poor in spirit" will answer "Yes" to the first eight questions and "No" to the last four.

Chapter 3

The Happy Mourners

"Blessed are those who mourn, for they shall be comforted."

—Matthew 5:4

Americans don't like to think sad thoughts. Dr. Darold Treffert, director of the Winnebago Mental Health Clinic in Winnebago, Wisconsin, says that the American fairy tale is that there are no problems. He notes that we consider it un-American if our children experience boredom, frustration, loneliness, or pain. He says we try to desensitize ourselves and one another to any unwanted feelings or experiences.

This hiding from problems is not new. Long ago false prophets were proclaiming "Peace, peace" when there was no peace (Jeremiah 6:14). God called this action a superficial healing which would not be healing at all (8:11). It is like trying to cover up the Grand Canyon with a Band-Aid.

Jesus said we need to mourn; and in that mourning we will find happiness and comfort. He congratulated the mourners, for through their mourning they would be buoyed up.

We were made in God's image and have the capacity to mourn. It's part of what being human is all about. The type of mourning Jesus was referring to cannot be done by animals or machines. God expects us to exercise our capacity to mourn.

Mourning—What Is It?

Jesus was certainly not telling the multitudes or us that we are to be continuous crybabies. The New Testament is filled with the word "joy," one of the fruits of the Spirit. Neither was Jesus suggesting that we be habitual pessimists. The world has enough people who think we are all on a giant "Titanic," going further down hourly. *Jesus was not commending the gloom and doom people, or the mad and sad folks.* He was not telling us to wipe off all our smiles and have no laughter in our worship services.

Jesus wants us to have life and have it *more* abundantly (John 10:10). He wants His joy to be in us, and our joy to be full (15:11). Our creator does not want us to have a *little* joy; He wants us to have *exceeding, great* joy! If the Wise-men who saw the star in the heavens could have that kind of joy (Matthew 2:10), then we who have experienced the Son should make their joy look meager. God wants us to prove the little girl wrong who said, when she saw a baboon for the first time, "He must be a Christian, because he has such a long face."

There are three words in the Greek language, used in the New Testament, for "mourn" or "grieve." One word *(lupe)* is a grief that does not have to be expressed; the person can hide it or hold it in. It will only be expressed when the person decides to do so.

Another word *(threnos)* is the grief that is expressed, but it may not be genuine. It may be a display of grief just for the "show" of it or for pay. It is done only because it is expected to be done. In Jesus' day many people were professional mourners. They were paid to mourn; the louder they wailed, the more they were paid.

The word that Jesus used *(penthos)* denoted the kind of grief that could not be covered up. It was a sincere sorrow that had to be shown. It was not the word used to mean being sad over everything that came along. This type of grief was restricted to specialized concerns.

It was a mourning over the following concerns: (1) a death (Genesis 23:2, etc.), (2) a separation caused by a son leaving a family (2 Samuel 13:37), (3) sorrow over sin or the results of sin—most often used in this way—(Numbers 14:39; 1 Samuel 15:35; 16:1; Nehemiah 1:4; Psalm 35:14; etc.).

While we are not to have this kind of grief over the physical death of a Christian (1 Thessalonians 4:13), *Jesus was saying that we are to mourn over those who are dead spiritually and over the sins that are so prevalent in our society.* We are to mourn over the results of sin in the lives of loved ones as well as over our own sins.

Mourning—Over What?
Our Own Sins

The child of God is poor in spirit, humbly realizing that he is spiritually bankrupt. He knows he is a sinner separated from God (Isaiah 59:2). He knows that sin brings eternal death and condemnation (Romans 6:23a).

But this knowledge and humbly crying out for help is not enough; mourning must soon follow. A child of God must also feel true sorrow for his sins.

His sorrow is not the human kind; that is, sorrow only because he got caught. Everyone is sorry when he gets caught in a sin, but not everyone is ready to decide never to repeat that sin. Many merely decide not to get *caught* at it again. Some even spend years in prison plotting how to commit the same sin without getting caught.

Instead, his sorrow is the godly kind; he is sorry for the hurt his sin has caused God and others. He is truly sorry for the pain sin causes.

Sin grieves God, not because He is above reality or is embarrassed by sin, but because it hurts those whom He has created and whom He loves so much. God hates sin because of the pain it causes, and we must hate it for the same reason.

If we are mourning correctly, we will not quit stealing just so we will go to Heaven, but we will quit stealing because that sinful action hurts someone else. Neither will we commit adultery, for it hurts others. We will not gossip because it hurts someone else. We will see ourselves as God sees us, and we will see the value that God places on every human being.

If we are mourning as Jesus said we must, we will take personal responsibility for our sins, confess them to God, and repent from them— determined not to repeat them. The prodigal son is a good example of a person who realized he had hit rock bottom (poor in spirit), saw his own sin, took responsibility for it, saw how it had hurt others, and turned away from it. He returned home, saying, "Dad, I've hurt you. I'm sorry. I want to serve you the rest of my life." He was mourning in the correct sense.

We must continually be sensitive to our own sins; it is not a onetime action or attitude. God's people in the Old Testament were specially chosen and were God's children, but they became hardhearted and insensitive to their own sins. They procrastinated repentance; they rationalized rebellion; they soft-soaped sensuality; and they wallpapered over their dishonesty and cruelty.

We can also become insensitive to our sins unless we remain constantly alert to the dangers. God has provided each of us with an internal alarm system that makes a racket when we sin—it is called "conscience." Our consciences work like little umpires who shout "foul" or "strike" when we goof. But, of course, we can soften the sound of the alarm or ignore the shouts of the umpire. Each time we do, we become a little less senstitive to that sin. Before long, the alarm does not even go off; the umpire decides not to shout at all. Our conscience becomes weak (Romans 8:7), and we lose consciousness of sin.

One way to sharpen our sensitivity to sin is the habitual gathering of God's people. That continual fellowship can serve to deter us from sin and help us sharpen our awareness of sin (Hebrews 10:24-26). But, of course, just attending the services is not enough. We need to open our hearts and ears to feel and hear the admonishing, the encouragement, and the help (1 Thessalonians 5:14). When was the last time a sermon or lesson broke your heart? Or were you too busy criticizing the speaker?

Sins of Others

Still it is not enough to mourn over our own sins; we must also mourn over the sins of others. Paul criticized the Corinthians because they were aware of sin in their midst but were not mourning (1 Corinthians 5:2). Instead they were tolerating it.

We Christians need to look out for one another. We need to do for one another spiritually what Abraham did for Lot physically. Lot had been captured while in the city of Sodom. Abraham could have said, "He deserves it. He chose to live in that sinful place. He's made his bed, now let him lie in it." Instead Abraham went on a campaign to rescue Lot, footing all the bills and endangering his own life (Genesis 14).

Jesus did the same for us. We were captured by Satan, but Jesus came and rescued us at His own expense. We must do the same for our spiritual kinfolk who get captured by Satan's devices. We need to develop the kind of sensitivity that compels us to go rescue them. We should be willing to go anywhere at our own expense to help another who may be flirting with the devil's schemes.

However, it is not enough to mourn for only the sins of Christians; we must also mourn over the sins of the lost—the very basis of evangelism.

It is hard to understand why it is so difficult to stimulate people in the church to become involved in evangelism. We don't have to prod them to yell at a small child who is playing in the middle of the street when a car is coming. They may not even know the child, but they see the danger and will act upon it. They don't turn aside and say, "That is his business." So why don't we do something when we see people playing with sin and all Hell is bearing down upon them?

Perhaps our doctrine about sin is deficient. Do we realize the stinging devastation of sin? A sinner is bound for Hell; he will die in his own sin (John 8:24). Jesus is the *only* way to the Father and Heaven (John 14:6). We must not sugarcoat sin or explain it away, or else people will not recognize it or take responsibility for it. We must not say that there may be other ways to reunite with God, or we will be giving people a false sense of security.

We who are God's people today must not allow our current society to dictate to us what is and what is not sin. If the Bible says it is sin, then it is sin—even if every man, woman, and child disagree. Paul's words are still in effect.

> Or do you not know that the unrighteous shall not inherit the kingdom of God? Do not be deceived; neither fornicators, nor idolaters, nor adulterers, nor effeminate, nor homosexuals, nor thieves, nor covetous, nor drunkards, nor revilers, nor swindlers, shall inherit the kingdom of God.
>
> —1 Corinthians 6:9, 10

Sin is not something we vote on. It is something we must flee from. Run and run fast!

Sins of Society

Not only should we mourn over our own sins and those of others, but we must mourn over the sins of a nation. Jesus considered the sins of an entire category of people and denounced them with many woes (Matthew 23). If we are ready to stand with Jesus and denounce various sins of a people, then we must also be ready to weep with Him over our Jerusalem (Matthew 23:37).

But Jesus did not just denounce and then weep and stop there. He went into the city and began to do some sweeping out of the vileness (Luke 19:41-46). To be truly sensitive to the sins of our society, we must do something about cleaning up the mess sin leaves in its path. Evil will triumph if good men do nothing.

The most effective way to clean up the mess is by evangelism, but other methods are also needed. The porno movie houses and bookstores need to be closed. The literature our children are required to read in public schools needs to be monitored. Massage parlors need to be shut down. Drug outlets need to be exposed. Some television programs need to be terminated. Christians are not only to love that which is good, but they are also to hate that which is evil and do something to get rid of it.

Comfort—the Result of Mourning

The child of God mourns rightly, and he will allow for the mending of his soul and the mending of his environment. The mending that mourning brings will result in comfort, happiness, and a buoyancy of life.

We will be comforted *now* when we mourn over our sins and allow our lives to be mended by forgiveness. God is in the forgiving business. God has never been in the habit of locking people up into their past blunders. He has always delighted in picking up the broken pieces of humanity and forming them into a beautiful mosaic. His action could be compared to a stained-glass window which is made up of broken, irregular, jagged pieces. But when the pieces are molded together, they make a beautiful prism for the sunlight to pass through. And so it is with a broken life that allows the light of God's Son to shine through it.

We can only experience true joy after we have been convicted of our sin, taken the responsibility for it, and then know and feel the sweet and abiding comfort of God's forgiveness. This is the comfort that lasts because it is from Christ. It is not from education but from the Emmanuel; it is not from society but from the Savior; it is not from the government but from God.

God's comfort not only gives us joy, but it also changes us. We remain sensitive to sin and reach out to help others caught in its grasp. We remain afloat even though the sins of society try to drown us. We are mourning, but we are not miserable. We are instead comfortable and secure in God's love.

Our comfort is not all in the here and now. We will also be comforted when Jesus Christ comes again. The ones who were sensitive enough to sin to wash their robes in the blood of the Lamb (Revelation 7:14; 22:14) will experience comfort:

And He shall wipe away every tear from their eyes; and there shall no longer be any death; there shall no longer be any mourning, or crying, or pain; the first things have passed away.

—Revelation 21:4

Check Your Character*

	Yes	No

1. When you sin, do you go to the other person and ask for forgiveness?
2. Do you think about the hurt that sin brings to God and others when you are tempted?
3. Is your conscience as sensitive as it used to be?
4. Have you ever gone to a person who was caught in sin's clutches in an effort to bring him back to God?
5. Have you ever spoken out against the sins that are prevalent in your community?
6. Have you presented the gospel to a non-Christian?
7. Do you really believe that sin will send a sinner to a literal Hell?
8. Can you think of a sin that does not bother you as much as it used to?
9. Do you watch television programs that glamorize violence, sex, etc.?
10. Do you enjoy hearing gossip?

*The one who mourns will answer "Yes" to the first seven questions and "No" to the last three.

Chapter 4

Who Is in Control?

"Blessed are the gentle, for they shall inherit
the earth."

—Matthew 5:5

On Amy's fifteenth birthday she made the first
"B" she had ever made in her life. For most people to make a "B" would have been great, but
Amy had always been a straight "A" student.
Amy came home from school that day and
hanged herself. She left this note: "Mom and
Dad, you have never said anything to me about
having to get good grades. In fact, we rarely talk
about it. But I know you do not want nor could
you tolerate a failure. And if I fail in what I do, I
fail in what I am. Good-bye." Amy did not know
how to handle a failure.

Out of Control

All of us, as humans, tend to react negatively
to problem situations. One common reaction is
to give up: "I can't handle it. Everything is too
threatening." We tend to see ourselves as grass-
hoppers and our failures or problems as giants
that are about to squash us.

From this feeling of impending defeat, we may
react in one of two ways. One way is to withdraw
from the reality of the defeat. We can withdraw
mentally by spending most of our time day-

dreaming or hallucinating. Or we may withdraw physically by becoming a social dropout. Or we might withdraw morally by living in continual sin. Or we might withdraw permanently by committing suicide.

Another way we seek to escape failure is to retaliate. We want to go down fighting. Our weapons might be our tongues or our fists. We lash out in our hurt and pain, hoping our pain will go away if we inflict pain on others.

These types of reactions can lead to massacre and self-destruction. We can all remember the sixties in which the battle cry was, "Burn baby burn." The torch of massacre was lit and touched college campuses, governmental buildings, and entire sections of cities. Policemen and firemen who tried to help were shot. During this same period of time, the suicide rate rose alarmingly. Many felt the uselessness of the violence, and feeling there was no other alternative they killed themselves.

These tactics for escaping our failures are not new. On one occasion James and John wanted to burn a whole village—the cats, the dogs, the babies, everybody—in order to wipe out the prejudices which those people felt against them (Luke 9:51-54). They felt that was the way to take care of the sins of society.

Judas has been embezzling funds throughout the ministry of Jesus (John 12:4-6), and he even turned over his Master to the authorities to gain money (Matthew 26:14-16, 47-49). He was sorry for the sins he had committed (Matthew 27:3, 4), but to escape he hanged himself (27:5).

One of Jesus' other disciples sought to wipe out the sins of another by using force. He tried to thrust his sword into one of the soldiers who came to take Jesus, but he missed and whacked off his ear instead (Mark 14:47).

Godly Control

Jesus made clear to us in the Beatitudes that we are to recognize our failures (poor in spirit), that we are to take responsibility for our failures and mourn them, and that we are to remain calm and in control:

> "Blessed are the gentle (meek)."
> —Matthew 5:5

The word "meekness" pictures an inner attitude that results in controlled reactions. The original word is related to two Gothic words which mean to love *(fryon)* and to be a friend *(freund)*. Meekness is the quality of being a loving friend when faced with unpleasant circumstances. The Greeks used the word to describe *soothing* things: *smooth* winds, *tame* animals, and *calm* people.

"Meekness" was commonly used to describe a wild animal that had been domesticated. A wild horse is aggressive, harsh, and inconsiderate. He kicks when he wants to kick and bucks when he wants to buck. His spirit is out of control.

But when a wild horse is "broken," he does not become useless and weak; he becomes useful and controlled. He surrenders himself to another; he allows a person to control him. He puts himself under the rule and the reins of a master.

He becomes obedient to a bit and bridle. A *meek* horse will allow the spurs to cut deeply into his sides without bucking. He will not fight back when things don't go his way.

It is much the same with a meek person. He is not wild and uncontrolled, but mild—yet not a milk toast. He is calm, but not a coward. He is congenial, but not a compromiser. He is sweet, but not shy. He is easy going, but not an "easy touch." He is even tempered, but not timid. He is gentle, but not gullible. *He keeps his composure even when he is criticized, coerced, contradicted, confined, or conspired against.*

Meekness is the mark of wisdom from above (James 3:17). It is characteristic of the Holy Spirit (Galatians 5:22, 23). Jesus said He himself had the attitude of meekness:

> Take My yoke upon you, and learn from Me, for I
> am gentle (meek) and humble in heart.
> —Matthew 11:29

But we cannot say that Jesus was a pushover. He was a man's man in His humanness. He knew how to blast the Pharisees and how to clean the temple of wickedness. Yet He was no bully. He had all power and authority, but He never abused it.

The meek win over the monsters; the mild win over the mad. The calm win over the clamorous. Meekness is power, harnessed but effective. Violence will never make one the ruler of the whole universe. But the meek Lamb did become such a ruler (Philippians 2:9-11; Revelation 5:13; 11:15).

Of course, the world has a tough time with this message. The world does not think of being meek in the face of opposition or disappointment; the world thinks using brute force is the only way. Aggressiveness, self-assertion, cold steel, and the clenched fist are glamorized.

The world is caught up in the "survival of the fittest" mentality. But such a philosophy is not survival at all; it is really extinction. When a person or a nation gets exterminated, only the survivor is left—alone in alienation from God, from self, and from others. That type of survival leads to destruction.

So what do we do when we recognize we are spiritually bankrupt and are truly sorry and repentant? We don't withdraw from our failures, nor do we retaliate against ourselves or others. Jesus was saying, "Get control of yourselves. Don't go off half-cocked. Don't explode. Calm down."

Peter denied Jesus three times. He recognized he had done wrong and mourned over it (Matthew 26:75). He allowed the Lord to pick up the pieces of his troubled soul, and later he accepted the challenge to feed God's sheep (John 21:15-17). He spoke boldly before the same type of people who had crucified Christ (Acts 2). He even charged the Supreme Court of that day with murder (Acts 4:10, 11). He refused to be silenced by any human authority (4:19, 20; 5:40-42).

A few years ago a Christian psychiatrist told me about a beautiful teenage girl who tried to commit suicide. After several months in the psy-

chiatric ward of a hospital, the doctors con-
cluded that she felt she was a total failure morally. She knew she was evil and felt extremely
sorry about it. She wanted to start all over; she
felt the only way to do that was to kill her old self
so she could be born again.

Yes, Jesus said we should be born again, but
the rebirth does not come after a physical death.
It comes after a spiritual turnaround. It comes
from surrendering our wild nature to the bit and
bridle of the Master. We confess to Him and
calmly accept His acceptance of us.

*This surrendering ourselves to the control of
the Master is not a onetime action; we must sur-
render daily in order to progress toward Christlikeness.*

The Affliction

Not only should we react with meekness in
reaction to our own sins and failures, but also to
the sins of others—especially when those sins
have been directed toward us personally. I am
sure we all realize that in this circumstance
meekness is very difficult to put into practice.
Most of us can get quite feisty when our feathers
get ruffled by someone else's offenses—
especially when we don't deserve the rough
treatment. Life often has a way of placing us on
the wrong end of the stick, doesn't it?

In one sense, there is no such thing as a meek
attitude or behavior pattern unless there is some
type of torment present. Without adversity our
calmness is nothing more than inactivity. We can
only respond meekly if there is some type of fric-

tion. That is probably why the word "meekness" is sometimes translated in the Old Testament as "afflicted" (Psalm 147:6; 149:4).

What should we do when afflicted? We should take it as Jesus did. He could even pray, "Father forgive them." We should forgive those who afflict us, and forgiving involves forgetting (Hebrews 8:12). God remembers to forget, and so should we. We can forget how others afflict us by practicing the following:

1. Do not respond negatively to another's offenses. It is tough but remember how Jesus remained calm and quiet throughout the verbal and physical abuses of His trial.

2. Never defend yourself verbally. Let others do it. If no one does, then perhaps your action does not need defending. The more you seek to defend yourself either publicly or privately, the more embittered you will become.

3. Don't go around telling others how someone offended you. Every time you repeat it, you will be reliving it and impressing it more upon your memory.

4. Throw away all letters or other evidence of how the person mistreated you.

5. Forgive the person—both in your mind and in your treatment of that person socially.

6. Go to the person, tell him you forgive him, and ask him to accept that forgiveness. If you do not take this important step, that person will not know that your mind and attitude have cleared him of the mistake. Everytime he sees you, he will think there is a barrier between you and him. He will wonder what you are thinking about him.

If you treat him nicely, he will think you are putting up a front. You must tell him that the barrier is removed; that you have forgiven and forgotten.

7. Socially interact with that person as soon as possible—go out to eat or to a ballgame together.

8. Think of all the positive things about that person and repeat them to others.

Meekness is the mark of a mature Christian. Actions of Christian maturity include the following behavior patterns. I'm sure you will note how closely they are related to meekness:

> Be angry, and yet do not sin; do not let the sun go down on your anger.
> —Ephesians 4:26

> Bearing with one another, and forgiving each other, whoever has a complaint against any one; just as the Lord forgave you, so also should you. And beyond all these things put on love.
> —Colossians 3:13, 14a

> Make friends quickly with your opponent.
> —Matthew 5:25

> And if any one wants to sue you, and take your shirt, let him have your coat also.
> —Matthew 5:40

This is not to say that the meek person gives in to every demand that comes along. Paul appealed to Caesar instead of letting the Jerusalem lynch mob take him. Peter never let the leaders in the court shut him up. Paul never surrendered right teachings to allow wrong practices to continue in the churches. Jesus never allowed the people around Him to squeeze Him into their

43

molds. Moses was called meek (Numbers 12:3), but he did not give in to the Pharaoh or let the idolatry and rebellion of the Hebrews weaken his convictions and communication to them.

But none of these people ever trampled others under their feet either. They acted calmly and with self-control. If opposition came, they took it without a spirit of vengeance. Some were killed without uttering one word of bitterness.

Remember Stephen? As the angry mob was stoning him, "He cried out with a loud voice, 'Lord, do not hold this sin against them!' And having said this, he fell asleep" (Acts 7:60). What meekness! What control!

The Inheritance

The meek child of God is even more in control than he can ever imagine. For Jesus said,

> Blessed are the gentle (meek), for they shall in-
> herit the earth.
> —Matthew 5:5

The meek are in charge of a vast inheritance. As joint heirs with Christ, the meek share in His honor and glory; they share in owning all that belongs to God. The meek are in high places with Christ Jesus (Ephesians 2:6).

Knowing this truth ought to enable us to remain meek. We don't have to get uptight with someone who is cheating us. We don't have to assert ourselves. There is no need to "pull our own strings," for we have surrendered to the Master and we jointly own the entire universe. We own all the gold in Fort Knox; the seven wonders of the world; as well as Niagara Falls.

Meek is not weak. It is power; it is control. It is a change of character and conduct. The riches of the world will change hands. Congratulations to the meek, for they will inherit the earth! The meek can keep afloat no matter what, because they know what is in their future and they know Who is in control.

Check Your Character*

	Yes	No
1. Do you get angry easily?		
2. Do you yell at your family repeatedly?		
3. Do you verbally criticize others often?		
4. Do you often say things you are sorry you said?		
5. Do you quarrel with others a lot?		
6. Do you enjoy finding other's mistakes?		
7. Do you defend yourself vehemently when you are misunderstood?		
8. Do you remember the wrongs done to you?		
9. Do you insist on having the last word in every situation?		
10. Are you known as the "calm" person in the midst of tension?		
11. When you do get angry, are others surprised?		

*Those who are meek will answer "No" to the first nine questions and "Yes" to the last two.

Chapter 5

No Saturation Point

"Blessed are those who hunger and thirst for
righteousness, for they shall be satisfied."
—Matthew 5:6

When I was in the military service, it was always a joy to come home and taste Mom's cooking. I had many varied experiences with food, and in many different countries, yet when I came home on leave and Mom asked what I would like to eat, I would always ask for three things: potato soup, oyster stew, and pecan pie. Mom's homemade potato soup was better than a filet mignon any day. Regardless of who we are, what we have done, or where we have gone, nothing tastes quite as good as the food on Mom's table. Wives have a tough time accepting that fact, but there should be no mystery. Our physical appetites were developed by the one who first fed us and kept feeding us during our growing-up years.

Restaurants know this fact and use it to their advantage. They advertise "homemade soup" and "homemade pie." They will always sell more soup and pies that way, because homemade cooking adds just the right personal touch.

Having an appetite and eating foods are everyday occurrences, and one of the marks of healthy living. The person who has no appetite is sick. Unless he regains his appetite, he will die.

A Spiritual Appetite

Jesus talked about the necessity for a spiritual appetite when He said:

> Blessed are those who hunger and thirst for righteousness.
>
> —Matthew 5:6

The Greek words for "hunger" *(peinao)* and "thirst" *(dipsao)* describe a demanding desire, a compelling craving, a wrestling wish. The Greeks did not use these words to describe only the desire for physical food and drink, for they realized that people can hunger and thirst after *anything*.

What we really desire, wish for, and crave after tells a lot about the real persons we are. Our appetites tell something about our attitudes. Our desires demonstrate something about our demeanor. Our wishes reveal something about our whole being. Our cravings point out something about our characters.

Hungering and thirsting come on the heels of a famine or a fast. A person feels a real pain, a real need for nourishment. Jesus hungered *after* He had fasted forty days (Matthew 4:2). It was *after* He had traveled for several hours that He thirsted (John 4:1-7). It was *after* the people had been with Jesus for hours or days that they hungered (Matthew 14:15; 15:32).

The hungering and thirsting person recognizes that he has a spiritual lack. He notices a painful deficiency. But just recognizing the spiritual need is not enough. This Beatitude shows us the way to the real solution to the sin situation— hungering and thirsting for righteousness.

47

God's Menu

To fulfill his need, a hungering and thirsting person will have to admit that he must depend upon some outside supply source. The arrogant, self-made person who is closed off from outside aid will starve to death. There must be humility along with the hungering and thirsting.

The hungering and thirsting person must also be ready to receive. He won't be the type who will refuse to eat because the menu did not have on it what he expected. Many people decide ahead of time all the details of salvation and then do not want to accept God's revealed solution.

The Jews had this attitude for years. They had their own idea of the Messiah, and they had the terms for salvation already worked out in their minds. They were looking for God to put a stamp of approval on their theology. But they forgot who it was that was hungry. God was not hungering and thirsting for their solution. He was not looking for the best manufactured scheme for salvation. He had already diagnosed man's need and designed His menu to take care of it.

But it takes a real hunger and thirst to eat of God's menu, because it is so nontraditional. The Jews could not accept it. They could not even stomach the head chef that God sent—Jesus. They wanted Him removed from their lives, so they killed Him.

Man has often gone after the fulfilling of his desires with much the same mentality as Naaman, the mighty commander of the Syrian army. He was hungering to be healed of leprosy, but he balked at God's solution of washing seven times in the Jordan River (2 Kings 5:1-11). He thought his own provisions were better (5:12). He wasn't humble enough to lay aside his own scheme to taste of God's menu at first. But when his mistake was pointed out to him, he dipped seven times in the "inferior" water and was healed (5:13, 14).

Not being hungry enough to take what God offers on His terms will lead to eternal starvation—damnation. That happens when a person believes that he can be well fed apart from God's menu:

> Woe to you who are well-fed now, for you shall be hungry.
>
> —Luke 6:25

Feeding Self

A person who hungers and thirsts will not just sit in the pantry and say, "I'm hungry and thirsty and dying by the minute." He will be motivated to do something about his hunger and thirst.

God knew physical hunger was a motivating force, and so He inspired Paul to say, "If anyone will not work, neither let him eat" (2 Thessalonians 3:10). Such a stipulation was surely a stimulation to get them off their comfortable porches.

True hungering and thirsting will result in action. We may know that food is available, but we must do something to receive it. When Paul recognized his starvation status, he cried out, "What shall I do, Lord?" (Acts 22:10). Jesus did not reply, "Just rock in your rocking chair." Paul did something about his hunger pains; he did as

Jesus directed. Thus he did not starve to death spiritually. In fact, he started serving others the banquet of God's menu, His Word, which not only saved them from death, but it warmed and filled them with the fruit of the Spirit. What a turnaround!

Feeding Others

Yes, it is the hungry and the thirsty who have really felt the pains of deprivation that can reach out and fulfill the needs of others. We are saved from our starvation to serve others in theirs. We were helped in our hunger and thirst in order to help others in theirs.

That is why the church is referred to as branches of a tree—we are to bear fruit. For centuries God's people have been likened to vineyards because they are to bear good, eatable grapes (Isaiah 5).

There is a modern parable that illustrates this point rather well. A man was traveling through a hot, dry desert. For many days he had gone without water. His mouth was dry, parched, and felt like it was glued shut. He was nearly dead when he arrived at an oasis. To his surprise he found a gallon of water in a sealed container next to the water pump. Tied to the container was this note: "Don't drink this water!" His heart sank, but he read on, "Use all of this water to prime the pump. Then use the first water that comes out of the pump to refill this container. You will then have all the water you want. And so will the travelers that come after you."

Jesus expects His people—the church—to

feed those who are hungering and thirsting (Matthew 25:31-46; Acts 2:44-47; 2 Corinthians 8, 9). Feeding others is the God-appointed function of the church, and Jesus expects her to fulfill it. We are to have compassion for those who are starving physically as Jesus did (John 6:1-21), but we cannot stop there. We must also be interested in feeding those who are in spiritual need (John 6:22-59).

God made our function clear in the Old Testament when He condemned the leaders of God's people (shepherds) because they fed themselves, but neglected to feed their sheep (Ezekiel 34:2). When the sheep got hungry, they wandered all over the place (34:6). Consequently, they became a prey for devouring beasts of pagan doctrines and experiences (34:5).

People who are really hungry and thirsty will eat and drink *anything*. Let's be sure they are fed the "bread of life" (John 6:35) and given the "living water" to drink (John 7:37-39).

It is our commitment to feed others that spreads the influence of the Christian community in quantity and deepens it in quality. The church matures partly by the reservoir of what those who have gone on before us have left for us to draw from.

I have seen the same principle manifest itself in our immediate family. Each one of our children caught on to the various experiences and expressions of life faster than the child before. Our youngest is three years old as I write this. She is far ahead of the other children at the same age in her speech and in her comprehension of what is going on about her. Why? Largely because each one of our other children have shared their experiences with her. And because she has been open to learn from them. This same principle should be at work within the church.

One of the great wastelands in Christianity is the tendency of so many Christians to take in but not give out. Many sit for hours under special instruction, but have never taught others. We should all attend special seminars, conventions, classes, etc., not to be counted or to bring attention to ourselves, but in order to be able to feed the hungering and thirsting people all around us.

Don't Get Full

Our hungering and thirsting as children of God is not a onetime episode. It is to be an ongoing craving. It must never stop in this earthly lifetime. Luke recorded Jesus saying, "Blessed are you who hunger *now*" (6:21). The "now" is a continuing now. It is to always be present. We should always be aware that we are not full. We should always be ready to be fed by God's Word and other Christians. And we should always be sensitive to the needs of others and be ready to feed them.

To lose the hunger would be to regress. It would be a loss of appetite that would result in spiritual starvation. We would lose "spiritual weight"; we would become anemic and unable to function properly.

To feel "filled up" would be to close ourselves

off to others. The Christians in Corinth experienced that very thing. They became satisfied with their level of Christianity.

> You are already filled, you have already become rich, you have become kings without us.
> —1 Corinthians 4:8

Their self-satisfaction stifled their growth toward maturity. They thought they had taken in enough nourishment and had already reached maturity. However, they had really blocked the growth process and were functioning as babies (1 Corinthians 3:1-3) which accounted for all of their internal problems.

How about you? Are you still hungry and thirsty? Are you still learning? Are you still reading the Word? Are you still listening to others? Are you constantly changing and maturing? Or do you still believe the same as you did ten years ago? Be careful if you think you are filled! You may think you are a forty-year-old Christian, but you might be a one-year-old Christian who has relived that first year forty times over. Are you really progressing?

To be continuously hungry and thirsty spiritually means we are open to continual fellowship, to prayer, to the breaking of bread, and to the apostles' teachings (Acts 2:42). A continuing hunger and thirst motivates us to nourish ourselves so we can grow on to maturity, and to nourish others so they can grow also.

At the same time, we must remember that we will always have an appetite for something. In that fact lies potential danger for the Christian.

The devil uses our appetites to tempt us. All of us are tempted when we are lured and enticed by our own desires or appetites (James 1:13, 14). God gave us all of our basic desires—for food, drink, security, sex, etc. God also gave us a wonderful world in which to fulfil those desires. He also gave us the guidelines about *how* those desires were to be met.

Satan uses those desires and the same world to lure and entice us to satisfy those desires outside of God's guidelines. It is as if we were traveling down a curving, mountainous road (life), but we are protected by the guardrails at the side of the road (God's guidelines). As long as we stay on the right side of the guardrails, we will be alright. But Satan wants us to venture out beyond the guardrails. If we do, our destruction is imminent.

The Food

For what should we be hungering and thirsting? For righteousness! The righteousness of Jesus who is the "Righteous One" (Acts 3:14; 22:14; 1 John 2:1; 3:7). But that type of food takes some getting used to. The hunger and thirst for it must be continually developed.

When I first tasted pizza, I sort of liked it. But the more I ate it, the more I liked it. I developed a taste for it. Now I love it. In much the same way we must develop a continuous appetite for Christlikeness.

We may sort of like the idea at first. But the more we actually practice it, the more we will come to love it and realize it is the way to fulfillment. Being like Jesus is much like returning home to our Mom's cooking. We were created in the beginning in His likeness. And when we become Christians, we are returning to that image—the menu that God prepared for us from the start.

Staying hungry and thirsty in this way requires more than just "tasting" Christianity. It requires keeping our appetites on the right things continually.

Check Your Character*

                                 Yes No

1. Do you keep a regular schedule of Bible reading?
2. Do you try to fellowship with God's people every time you possibly can?
3. Do you read Christian books regularly?
4. Do you read Christian periodicals regularly?
5. Have you attended special classes or seminars to increase your knowledge and appreciation of God and His Word?
6. Do you attend the worship service only on Sunday morning because you feel that is "enough"?
7. Do you allow a television program to keep you home from church activities?

*The hungering person will answer "Yes" to the first five questions and "No" to the last two.

Chapter 6

The Right Meal

"Blessed are those who hunger and thirst for
righteousness, for they shall be satisfied."
—Matthew 5:6

Have you ever looked at a printed menu in a
restaurant and wondered what you were reading? Have you ever asked yourself, "Wonder if I'll
like that?" or "I wonder how that dish is made?"
or "I wonder if this meal will be satisfying?"

Similar questions would probably be asked
in the spiritual realm if we would say, "I wonder
if I'll like a meal of righteousness?" or "How do I
get filled on righteousness?" or "I wonder if righteousness will be truly satisfying?"

Reading the Menu

What does a meal of righteousness contain?
What is it made up of? How can I get it?

The Greek word for righteousness *(dikaiosune)*
is one of those "heavy" words used in twenty of
the New Testament books. The word was origi-
nally used to describe someone whose conduct
was lined up correctly with the set standards. He
would be similar to a train that stays on its
tracks. It lines itself up with the tracks and continues in that way in its everyday journey.

There are two "tracks" involved in righteousness: (1) our relationship with God and (2) our

relationship with each other. To ride on only one track would not result in righteousness. It would result in an unbalanced and thus precarious situation. A righteous person looks up to God and looks out for his fellowmen. If he does not stay on these two tracks consistently, he will derail.

We can think of our society as one long train racing toward its destination. Only righteousness can keep it on the right track.

But how can we get righteousness to become a part of our daily lives? The Jews thought that stacking up a good score on the ledger sheet, which would be tabulated by how many of the laws were kept, would automatically result in righteousness. However, Paul emphasized that righteousness does not come through the law (Galatians 2:21). In fact, one function of the law was to show man how *unrighteous* he was (Romans 7:7, 8).

In order to appropriate a meal of righteousness, we must know about its ingredients and how to assimilate them into our lives.

The Ingredients
A Pronouncement

Sin severs our relationship with God; a mending is needed. The only way for the mending to take place is if we are declared or *pronounced righteous*. God pronounces us righteous when we are convicted of our sin by the action of the Holy Spirit (John 16:8), and when we commit our lives to God because of the conviction. Only then will a right relationship with God be restored, no matter how good or moral we might be.

Cornelius was said to be a righteous man by human evaluations (Acts 10:22). He had so much going for him. It looked as if his relationship with both God and man was ideal (Acts 10:1-4, 22).

With God	With Man
devout	gave alms
feared God	well spoken of by
prayed continuously	Jews
saw an angel	

He was a man whose prayers and good deeds served as a memorial before God (Acts 10:4). But that was not enough. He was told to listen to Peter who would "speak words to you by which you will be saved" (11:14).

A man is not righteous in God's eyes until he has been pronounced righteous.

A Power

Righteousness is not restricted to that which comes to us externally. It also includes *a power within us* that begins to change us.

God as our judge does what no human judge can do. A human judge can pronounce the words "not guilty," but he cannot put within us an inner power to begin living out a new life. God declares us legally righteous and acquitted of our wrongs and then gives us the power to function as righteous persons. He declares us righteous and then designs us to be righteous in our conduct and character. He enables us to become new creations, new people.

Christ died so that we could have this righteousness, this new life:

> He made Him who knew no sin to be sin on our
> behalf, that we might become the righteousness
> of God in Him.
> —2 Corinthians 5:21

We actually become righteous because the
"Righteous One"—Jesus—comes to reside
within us:

> The gift of righteousness will reign in life
> through the One, Jesus Christ.
> —Romans 5:17

God justifies (makes righteous) those who
have faith in Jesus (Romans 3:26); and those
who have this faith express it in obedience (Galatians 3:26, 27). In Christ we begin a new life of
righteousness (Romans 6:4, 11, 13). To live in
righteousness is to live in Christlikeness.

The Assimilation

It is not easy to assimilate the Christlike
characteristics in God's meal of righteousness:

> For I say to you, that unless your righteousness
> surpasses that of the scribes and Pharisees, you
> shall not enter the kingdom of heaven.
> —Matthew 5:20

It is not easy to live out righteousness in our daily
lives; for the inner character must be matched
with the outer conduct. They both must be
matched with Christlikeness.

It is possible to pretend to be righteous (Luke
20:20; 2 Corinthians 11:14, 15). The Pharisees
were not the same on the inside as they were
on the outside. On the outside they were as
sheep; but on the inside they were as wolves

(Matthew 7:15). They looked clean on the outside, but inside they were filthy and perverted (Matthew 23:25-27). They appeared to be righteous, but on the inside they were lawless (23:28). They were not staying on the tracks in their journey of life.

We must seek for consistency. We must seek to have our inner life reflected by our outer life and vice versa. We want to look the same to God whether we are right side up or turned inside out or upside down.

Now let us move to the specifics. How will a righteous person act? We can look to Jesus for the example. He came to show us what God is like on the inside (John 1:18) by His words and actions on the outside. We can do the same (Matthew 5:16; 2 Corinthians 3:3; Ephesians 5:1).

In the rest of His Sermon on the Mount, Jesus listed in detail what a life of righteousness means and what an active faith entails: (1) be merciful (Matthew 5:7), (2) be pure in heart (5:8), (3) be peacemakers, (4) rejoice when persecuted (5:10-12), (5) preserve the good (5:13), (6) cause immorality to retreat (5:14-16), (7) control anger (5:21, 22), (8) be reconciled (5:23, 24), (9) do not lust after the opposite sex (5:27-30), (10) restrain from divorce (5:31, 32), (11) be faithful (5:33-37), (12) consider the welfare of others (5:38-42), (13) love your enemies (5:43-48), (14) worship to praise God (6:1-4), (15) pray to commune with God (6:5-13), (16) forgive others (6:14, 15), (17) be humble (6:16-18), (18) spend for God (6:19-24), (19) trust in God (6:25-34),

(20) realize your faults (7:1-5), (21) ask for help (7:7-12), (22) go the unpopular way (7:13-23), (23) act upon what you hear (7:24-27).

Jesus also demonstrated in His life many other aspects of righteousness. He never allowed His concern for spiritual purity to blind Him to the physical needs of others (Matthew 8). He never locked a man up into his past (9:9-13). He never saw a crowd as just another faceless mob, but He saw them as individuals with needs (9:35-38). He did not keep His disciples uninvolved or unequipped. He shared His work, methods, and abilities with them freely (Matthew 10). He honored a fellow worker (Matthew 11).

He never allowed human tradition to override taking care of people's needs (12:1-14; 15:1-21). He never let anyone detour His mission (12:15-50). He shared the truth (Matthew 13). We could go on and on emphasizing Jesus' righteousness.

It is *His* type of righteousness that we must hunger and thirst for, that we must desire, that we must crave. We must desire to be as mature as Christ (Ephesians 4:15). We must desire to abide in Christ (John 15); and we must desire to fellowship with God's people (Hebrews 10:23-25). We must desire to feed regularly on the Scriptures which are profitable for righteousness (2 Timothy 3:16, 17). We must desire to be disciplined (Hebrews 12:11). We must desire to give liberally of our material goods (2 Corinthians 9:7-10).

We must desire to be on the "front lines" in order to capture every thought to the obedience of Christ (2 Corinthians 10:5). We must be willing to be misunderstood and mistreated. We must obey God rather than men (Acts 4:19); we must do the Word as well as hear it (Romans 2:13). We must treat our employers or employees well (Colossians 3:22—4:1). We must think positive thoughts (Philippians 1:6, 7). We must not participate in unrighteousness (2 Corinthians 6:14-18). We must be good stewards (Luke 16:8), and we must care for others' needs (Matthew 25:37-40).

It is no wonder that Jesus said those who hunger and thirst after the lifestyle of righteousness are to be congratulated and will be buoyed up no matter what happens externally.

The Satisfaction

Jesus promised that the hungering and thirsting person who was seeking to make the lifestyle of righteousness his own would be satisfied (Matthew 5:6). The satisfaction is both in the present and in the future. God does not disappoint those who sincerely seek to become Christlike. He continually blesses Christians with His presence and the provisions of the Holy Spirit.

But the ultimate satisfaction will come when Jesus returns and grants us unrestricted exposure to the banquet hall in God's Heaven and to the "water of life" from which we will be eternally filled.

> And the Spirit and the bride say, "Come." And let the one who hears say, "Come." And let the one who is thirsty come; let the one who wishes take the water of life without cost.
> —Revelation 22:17

> They shall hunger no more, neither thirst any more; neither shall the sun beat down on them, nor any heat; for the Lamb in the center of the throne shall be their shepherd, and shall guide them to springs of the water of life; and God shall wipe every tear from their eyes.
> —Revelation 7:16, 17

> I will give to the one who thirsts from the spring of the water of life without cost.
> —Revelation 21:6

Let us eat of God's menu continuously, assimilate His ingredients daily.

Check Your Character*

	Yes	No

1. Have you expressed your faith in Jesus?
2. Do you increase your giving to the Lord each time your paycheck increases?
3. Do you evaluate everything you do by how Jesus would do it?
4. Is there someone whom you have not forgiven of an offense?
5. Are you more concerned about your outer conduct than you are about your inner thoughts and attitudes?
6. Are you a participating partner in any dishonest deal?
7. Have you ever cheated someone without making it right?

*The person who craves for righteousness will answer "Yes" to the first three questions.

Chapter 7

Making a Difference

"Blessed are the merciful, for they shall receive mercy."

—Matthew 5:7

Nobody wanted him. He was born with only one eye, no arms, no legs, and where his feet should have been there were two flippers. His mother had left him at the hospital where he remained for a long time.

When Andy was six years old, Hazel and Leonard heard about him. He was a pitiful sight when they first saw him, but they decided to become his friend. It was a real test to take him out to a restaurant and endure the disbelieving and astonished stares. But they did it. They fell in love with Andy and decided to adopt him.

Hazel and Leonard were no prizes themselves. Leonard made only $35 a week, and he was Hazel's third try at marriage. She was married in her teens, had a baby who died, had divorced, had an illegitimate child, and was a widow when Leonard met her. But they wanted to care for Andy.

When Andy found out about the adoption, he was so exuberant he shouted as Hazel carried him down the street in her arms, "I'm adopted! Yippee! I'm adopted!"

Hazel and Leonard showed mercy toward another who had a need. Andy received that mercy, and their lives were changed. Leonard was so concerned that Andy learn to navigate and do things for himself that he built a vehicle for him. Andy learned to operate the vehicle and could go around on his own muscle power. Others, learning of the vehicle and Andy's progress, asked Leonard to build vehicles for those who were handicapped in unusual ways. Leonard found a new business, Andy learned to live independently, and a loving family was formed. Mercy does make a difference.

The Inner Ache

What does it mean to be full of mercy? Mercy is both an inner feeling and an outer function. It begins on the inside but is shown on the outside.

Mercy is to "feel" with another's situation. It describes an inner feeling that comes from mentally crawling inside the skin of someone else, feeling his suffering or need. It is a *real* inward feeling, not a sham. Mercy is sympathy for the suffering, pity for the pitiful, compassion for the crushed, hurting with those who hurt.

The Outward Action

Mercy is an inner ache that is seen in an outer action. Of course, God is the perfect example of what the action of mercy involves. We were dead in our trespasses and sins; we were slaves to Satan; we were disobedient and enemies of God; we were indulging ourselves in selfish desires (Ephesians 2:1-3). God saw our misery and our hopeless predicament. He hurt with us. He felt mercy; and that mercy moved Him to allow His Son to become our substitute, to stand in for us, to take the punishment that we deserved.

Mercy is totally unearned and undeserved by us (Romans 9:16). We receive it as a gift. But we are not only to receive it, we are also to be merciful when dealing with others. We are to become vessels of God's mercy (9:23). God showed mercy *to* us partially in order to show mercy *through* us (11:31). We are to mirror God's mercy in our lives. This is not an option; this is a command.

The Recipients

To whom should we show mercy? We can look to Jesus for an example. Jesus' mercy was shown toward every kind of human misery—physical, spiritual, social, and ethnic. He cared for the hungry (Mark 8:1-8), the blind (Matthew 20:30ff; Mark 10:46ff; Luke 18:35ff), the demon-possessed (Mark 5:1ff; Matthew 15:22-28), the epileptic (Matthew 17:14ff), the leprous (Luke 17:11ff), those deeply in debt (Matthew 18:21ff), and for the terminally ill (Philippians 2:27). He extended mercy to women as well as men, the Greek as well as the Jew, the old as well as the young, the poor as well as the rich. Jesus' mercy was to the whole world and for the whole man. Our mercy is to be just as extensive as His was. Leading lives of satisfaction because we constantly seek righteousness does not give us the right to look down on anyone else. We are God's children only because of God's mercy, not because of any good we have done:

> For you once were not a people, but now you are
> the people of God; you had not received mercy,
> but now you have received mercy.
>
> —1 Peter 2:10

Meeting Spiritual Needs

Winning others is not a task assigned to just a few. All Christians are to be teaching the Word wherever they are and whatever they are doing:

> Therefore, those who had been scattered went
> about preaching the word.
>
> —Acts 8:4

In order to win others, we must be willing to become friends with and associate with sinners. Jesus made a special point to do that. He was criticized when He reached out to touch the untouchables of His society. When the religious do-gooders of His day saw that He spent time with the tax gatherers and sinners, they threw their verbal stones. It was in that context that He said, "I desire compassion" (Matthew 9:10-13). In that same passage, He made clear why He spent time fellowshipping with sinners: "It is not those who are healthy who need a physician, but those who are ill" (Matthew 9:12).

How would you react to a doctor who would not see your sick child until he got well, because the doctor did not want to be exposed to something that might be contagious?

The world is sick with sin and needs our sympathy, not our separation from it. People outside of Christ need our involvement in their lives, not our isolation from them.

For far too long we have pulled Scripture texts out of context to prove that we should have nothing to do with sinners. Every Scripture we use refers to our participating in the practices of sinners. No Scripture says we are not to associate with the people who sin. Paul made it clear that if we fail to associate with immoral people or non-Christians, then we might as well leave the world (1 Corinthians 5:9, 10). In this text, Paul was speaking about disciplining a fellow Christian.

Our teaching about Christ may not be heard or heeded if it is not accompanied by our caring and touching. We cannot evangelize people with whom we will not eat. We will find it difficult to save people with whom we will not socialize. The Pharisees' example taught us that isolationism is in opposition to God's ways.

> Woe to you, scribes and Pharisees, hypocrites, because you travel about on sea and land to make one proselyte; and when he becomes one, you make him twice as much a son of hell as yourselves.
>
> —Matthew 23:15

There will be no concern shown between people in Hell. And if we convert people to Christianity but teach them that they must withdraw all social contact with the lost, then we are teaching them to live out the lifestyle of Hell. Jesus indicted that approach then and still does today.

Jesus was criticized because He ate with sinners, just as you will be if you do so. Those with pointing fingers said, "This man receives sinners and eats with them" (Luke 15:1, 2).

In response to this criticism, Jesus told three parables; the significance of them is found in

68

understanding what they do *not* have in common:

(1) *The Lost Sheep.* A sheep was lost; the shepherd left the ninety-nine and sought the lost one. When he returned, he called in all his friends and neighbors to *rejoice* with him because he had found the lost sheep.

To one who lives in the city, this story may mean little. But suppose someone lost a four-wheeled animal—a Pinto, a Mustang, or a Cougar. What would he say if he stepped out of his apartment and his car was gone from the parking space? Would he say, "The Lord giveth and the Lord taketh away?" I doubt it. I suspect that owner would spend quite a bit of time and effort in a search, and he would rejoice greatly when it was found.

(2) *The Lost Coin.* A woman lost a silver coin. She searched carefully for it, and *everyone rejoiced* when she found it.

If it were a nickel or a dime, we would not expect that reaction. The silver coin in this parable (drachma) was a day's pay (before taxes). By the time you read this, the average day's pay in our country will probably be over $60. Would you just kiss sixty bucks good-bye? I doubt it. I imagine you would risk a cardiac arrest running after it or searching for it.

(3) *The Lost Son.* A person was lost in sin, but when he was found *not* everyone rejoiced. The elder brother was quite content as long as that scoundrel brother of his was far away and kept his distance. But he became angry and jealous when his brother was rescued and brought back into the family—he was getting too close!

Through these parables, Jesus was teaching that to God people are of much more value than possessions.

Our merciful actions will show what our value systems are.

A Modern Parable

If a stained-glass window in the church auditorium is broken on Monday, it would no doubt be fixed by Sunday. But what happens if a person's life gets broken on a Monday? Do we make sure that he gets patched up by Sunday?

Even Christians within the church have problems and needs. Some have fears and doubts. When they express them, some Christians begin to treat them as second class or as enemies. We need to show them mercy. Rather than give up on them, we must try to snatch them out of the fire (Jude 22, 23). That snatching process involves correcting them with gentleness (2 Timothy 2:24, 25).

Meeting Physical Needs

Mercy does not stop with the spiritual dimension; mercy extends to the whole person. As James said, benevolence is a legitimate demonstration of our faith (2:14-26).

> What use is it, my brethren, if a man says he has faith, but he has no works? Can that faith save him? If a brother or sister is without clothing and in need of daily food, and one of you says to them, "Go in peace, be warmed and be filled," and yet you do not give them what is necessary for their body, what use is that?
>
> —James 2:14-16

"Go in peace, be warmed and be filled" was probably a nice religious cliche which was heard often in the assembly; but no one moved to help. How many times have we prayed for the sick, the poor, or the unfortunate and never intended to do one thing to provide an answer to that prayer? That kind of religion turns God off (Isaiah 1:11-17). James told us that pure religion included looking after widows and orphans (1:27). Isn't it time we practiced the pure religion—the religion full of mercy?

Jesus emphasized that the needs of people are much more important than our keeping of religious traditions, especially those traditions which were and are being perpetuated by men (Matthew 12:1-8; Luke 11:11-13).

Is it possible that we are so busy keeping the religious machinery going that we have no time left over to care for the needs of others? Instead we leave the "caring" to civic clubs, governmental agencies, or special interest groups (such as Alcoholics Anonymous).

It was this same type of "busy-ness" that caused the two religiously-minded persons to walk on by the fellow who had been robbed, beaten, and left by the side of the road. I wonder if the Samaritan was on his way to a tavern when he stopped to help the poor fellow? He certainly knew where the nearest inn was, and he knew the proprietor well enough to tell him to put the expenses of caring for the man on his bill. Whatever the Samaritan's faith was or whatever his personal habits were, he felt compassion and extended mercy when it was needed. He applied medicine to the man's wound, bandaged him, put him on his donkey, took care of him in the inn, and paid for his further care (equal to two days' pay). Mercy takes time, effort, and sometimes money.

"Oh, no! Not money! I'll give time and effort, but don't ask me to give money!" One of the reasons Christians are to work in this life is so they can share monetarily with those who have physical needs (Ephesians 4:28).

If we would do this, I am sure we would constantly be more sensitive to the needs of those around us. We would even begin to actively "look" for opportunities to use our special fund.

It is possible to so institutionalize our religion that we expect the institution to look after the physical need of its members. We leave it to a committee to seek out the needs and meet them. The machinery of the church moves in this way, but without the proper motivation and often without the "personal" touch. When we don't get personally involved in deeds of mercy, but let the "church" do it, then we are keeping the wheels oiled while we ride on the running board. We are missing out on the real action and joy of Christianity. Let us remember that the well-oiled, well-organized machinery of a church does not impress God nearly as much as the sincere attitude and action of mercy.

Of course, people will oppose you if you expend energy and money to help relieve the physical needs of others. Jesus was criticized repeatedly for merciful actions (Matthew 15:22ff; 20:29ff; Mark 5; 10:46ff). It is interesting to note that we will be opposed if we express mercy evangelistically, and we will be opposed if we express mercy in benevolence. But if we let other people write our agenda, we will be paralyzed into doing nothing.

Jesus desires mercy, not a mulling over of a situation; He desires compassion, not just conferences; He desires serving, not just seminars that talk about serving. He wants our hands and heads to be converted along with our hearts.

The Responsibility

There is another side to the extension of mercy—the responsibility of those who receive mercy (and remember, we all fit into that category). People who receive mercy should *desire* to be helped. On at least three occasions Jesus mentioned the person's desiring to be helped:

> Be it done for you as you wish.
> —Matthew 15:28

> What do you wish?
> —Matthew 20:32

> Do you wish to get well?
> —John 5:6

The man in John 5:6 had been lame for thirty-eight years. Why would Jesus ask him such a foolish question? Wouldn't he want to get well? Not necessarily. Some people do not want to get out of their unfortunate situations. Some have learned that they can get more attention in their mess than if things were going well for them. Others realize that getting well will bring responsibilities with it that they are not ready to fulfill. A healed cripple would have to work for a living. Would he be ready for that?

The church has no obligation to help those who do not want it, and should not force it on them. Most of the people Jesus helped asked for the help (Matthew 9:27ff; 15:22ff; 17:14ff; 20:29ff; Mark 10:46ff).

Those who receive mercy must ponder *how to receive it* and *what to do with it* when they do. We must receive mercy with thanksgiving and not be like the nine lepers who forgot to give thanks (Luke 17:11ff). We also need to glorify God after receiving mercy (Romans 15:9). To glorify God means to characterize Him in our lifestyles. The finest way to praise and honor God is to seek to live like He wants us to—to imitate His characteristics, just as children imitate the characteristics of their parents.

The Reward

Jesus said a person who showed mercy was to be congratulated. He would be a buoyant person amidst difficulties because he would receive mercy (Matthew 5:7).

Jesus told a parable about a man who was in debt for 10,000 talents (equivalent to several million dollars today). When he expressed his regrets, his debt was canceled. But the same man refused to give another man any time to pay a debt he owed him (which was for much less money). Even though he had received mercy, he refused to extend mercy to someone else; and he was punished severely for it (Matthew 18:23-35).

Jesus' point was that whatever wrongs have been hurled at us are a mere drop in the bucket compared to how we have wronged God. If He can give us an entire ocean of forgiveness and mercy, then surely we can give a few drops of forgiveness and mercy to others.

The presence and practice of mercy will be a major consideration when Jesus returns on Judgment Day. Those who have fed the hungry, given drink to the thirsty, become a friend to the stranger, given clothes to the naked, taken care of the sick, and visited the prisoners will spend eternity in Heaven (Matthew 25:31-40).

The merciful will receive mercy both in this life and in the life to come. God will bless the merciful; He will allow us to sow bountifully and reap bountifully; He will multiply our resources (2 Corinthians 9:6, 10). He will consider our help to the poor to be a personal loan to Him which He will repay (Proverbs 19:17); His dividends will be greater than any present-day company's.

His final mercy is eternal life. What a dividend that is! We will never be able to spend it all; we will be able to enjoy it forever.

Yes, mercy changes lives—the lives of those who extend mercy and the lives of those who receive mercy. The changes are both current and eternal.

Check Your Character*

	Yes	No

1. Have you invited someone into your home for a meal in the past year who could not have

you in their home?

2. Do you really take time to help others (such as baby-sit for a young couple, take meals to a shut-in, or visit a widow)?

3. Have you talked to someone about your faith recently with the intent of helping them to become Christians?

4. Do you have any non-Christian friends?

5. Have you given money to anyone personally to help with a physical need?

6. Would you be willing to miss a worship service to look after the needs of another?

7. Do you set aside some money to help others in benevolent ways?

8. Can you name people who need to receive mercy?

9. Can you receive help from others without feeling inferior?

10. Have you received God's mercy by becoming a Christian?

11. Do you ever invite a poor family or a poor child into your home for a meal or entertainment? Or do something similar to this to extend your hand of fellowship?

*A person who is full of mercy will answer "Yes" to all of these questions.

Chapter 8

Cleaning Up

"Blessed are the pure in heart, for they shall see God."

—Matthew 5:8

The following is a popular but powerful story: Some Americans were on an around-the-world package tour. As they were visiting a leprous area in a remote section of a third-world country, they observed a missionary stooping over a miserable and wretched piece of humanity who was covered with open and oozing sores. The missionary was gently wiping away the infectious, yellow-white liquid that had a putrid odor. One American observed the action a few seconds, then walked away, muttering under his breath, "I wouldn't do that for a million dollars." The missionary whispered, "I wouldn't either."

That missionary was being pure in heart. He was not caring for the leper in order to get paid or to bring praise and honor upon himself. He was simply seeking to meet another's need.

The Pulse

Why we do what we do is as important as *what* we do. Are we doing good deeds and living right just to be noticed or to hear the praise of the crowds?

Being godly (being like God) requires a great deal of effort and time (and money sometimes). If we are being godly primarily for the compliments, then nothing would prevent us from throwing in the towel and quitting when the "applause" ceases. But if we do it with pure motives, we will remain steadfast when not appreciated. Our "pure in heart" motivations are the adrenalin that keeps the heart pulsating and keeps our lives balanced. They control our spiritual blood pressure, so we won't fly off the handle if things don't go our way or if we don't get recognition for what we do.

When the "pure in heart" motivation stops working, we experience a spiritual cardiac arrest. A "Code Blue" is sounded in Heaven. If the pulse is not resumed quickly, a further hardening of the spiritual arteries will set in to cement us into our old way of life. The Pharisees who tried had a tough time keeping the "pure in heart" pump working, which led to all their distortions of God's will. Their spiritual pulses were at a very low ebb, almost to extinction.

The Heart

When the Bible talks about the heart, it is not referring to any specific physical organ inside of man; neither is it speaking metaphorically of any one spiritual aspect hidden inside of man. The "heart" does not refer to a muscle-center, but to a motivating-center that makes the whole man do what he does. It is the source of a person's personality and behavior. It involves a combination of the intellectual, emotional, volitional, and spiritual foundations of a person. If these foundations are "off" or "unsettled," then the whole person will be "off" or "unsettled."

The Greeks used the word "heart" to refer to the "central power plant"—the central switchboard—that controls the whole person. Today we would probably use the word "mind" to say the same thing. The Bible uses the words "mind" and "heart" interchangeably as well. When Jeremiah said the heart was deceitful above all else, he was referring to the mind (Jeremiah 17:9, 10). Peter talked about having a pure mind (2 Peter 3:1) which would mean the same as being pure in heart.

In a larger sense, the "heart" is a description of the whole person—whatever it is that you are in your selfhood. To personalize the Bible's use of the word, you could insert the word "self" or "myself." To be pure in heart is to be pure in myself. To love God with your whole heart is to love Him with your whole self (Matthew 22:37).

To see clearly that the heart refers to the whole person, let us look at what the New Testament says the heart does: (1) the heart loves (Matthew 22:37), (2) the heart thinks (Matthew 5:28), (3) the heart is gentle and humble (Matthew 11:29), (4) the heart speaks (Matthew 24:48), (5) out of the heart comes evil (Matthew 12:34, 35), (6) the heart understands (Matthew 13:15), (7) the heart receives God's seed (Matthew 13:19), (8) the heart forgives (Matthew 18:35), (9) the heart reasons (Mark 2:6), (10) the heart hardens (Mark 6:52—makes decisions), (11) the heart believes or doubts (Romans

10:10), (12) the heart sets priorities (Luke 1:17), (13) the heart is troubled and sorrowful (John 14:27), (14) the heart worries (Luke 21:34), (15) the heart rejoices and is glad (John 16:22), (16) the heart is convicted (Acts 2:37), (17) the heart is tempted (Acts 5:3, 4), (18) the heart purposes (Acts 11:23), (19) the heart obeys (Romans 6:17), (20) the heart desires (Romans 10:1), (21) the heart houses the Holy Spirit (2 Corinthians 1:22), (22) the heart draws near to God (Hebrews 10:22), (23) the heart gives thanks and sings (Colossians 3:16), and (24) the heart calls upon the Lord (2 Timothy 2:22).

It is no wonder that the heart is referred to as the inner man (1 Peter 3:4). The heart describes what we really are on the inside. And out of that heart come our attitudes and our actions.

Purity

The Greek word "pure" *(katharos)* was used, first of all, to refer to something physically clean—such as a cloth that had no foreign matter clinging to it, or water with no pollution in it, or a metal that had nothing else mixed with it. Wheat was called "pure" when the chaff was removed. A person was medically pure (clean) when he had no disease (Matthew 8:2; 10:8; 11:5; Luke 17:14).

The Greeks understood that something was "pure" when it was free from additives. It described a special kind of "freedom." It was a freedom from anything that hindered the item from being what it was intended to be, or from being used in the way it was created to be used.

Water that poisoned rather than nourished was not free to be the water it was created to be. A cloth bandage that infected a wound rather than aided in healing was not free to be used as it was intended to be used. Something interfered. When the interference was removed, the item was freed to perform its intended usage—it was pure or clean.

A pure heart frees a person from all hindrances that would prevent him from being what God intended him to be. God created us in His image and likeness, but sin interferes with that image. The "pure in heart" child of God is freed from sin and does not allow sin to blockade his usefulness to God and others. Being pure in heart does not refer to just a past action, but to a continuing action.

The "pure in heart" person will live without any mixed motives. His speech and action will be sincere (purity and sincerity are synonymous—1 Peter 3:1; Hebrews 10:22). In fact, in the first century, people used the word "sincere" to describe a sculptured statue that had no niches plastered over. The flaws were openly exposed. Thus, purity came to refer to someone who wasn't trying to cover up his real motives. He would say what he meant and mean what he said. He did not speak or act with "tongue in cheek." When he signed a letter "sincerely," he meant there were no hidden meanings in the words.

To be "pure in heart" is the opposite of being double-minded (having two motives). Do you ever speak or act with hidden motives? Do you ever say what you think others want to hear rather than what they need to hear? Do you ever claim to understand when you really don't, because you don't want to appear stupid? Do you ever fake sadness or happiness? Do you ever do something helpful in order to get attention drawn to you? All of these are examples of double-mindedness.

Let us consider some other examples: (1) When you answer someone's question about how you are feeling with a "Fine!" when you feel rotten. (2) When you say, "We need to get together," or "You must come see us" when you do not intend to do either. (3) When you change what you say you believe depending on the group of people you are with. (4) When you make a promise intending to forget it. Such vacillation is not being "pure in heart."

> Double-mindedness leads to instability.
> —James 1:8
> (paraphrase)

Have you ever felt that your mind was pulled in two different directions? I felt that way for a time in my life. I was in one profession but desired to be in another. I went through a period of mental agony before I resigned my job to study to become a preaching minister. When I took that step, my double-mindedness turned into a single-mindedness. I had a purpose and was determined to achieve it. I was no longer ambiguous; I committed myself wholeheartedly to the task. That is the same characteristic as being "pure in heart." All the hindrances are put aside; the one goal looms ahead; all the efforts are in aiming toward that goal; and stability in a person's attitude and behavior reigns.

The Pharisees missed what "pure in heart" meant. They put all their emphasis upon a person keeping the ritualistic traditions. If he performed all the rituals, he was "clean." They evaluated all people only by externals.

That is why the Pharisees had such a tough time with Jesus' behavior. If He ate nontraditional food, failed to wash His hands after having touched a Gentile, or did something on the Sabbath day, they considered Him unclean and publicly criticized Him:

> Why do Your disciples transgress the tradition of the elders? For they do not wash their hands when they eat bread.
> —Matthew 15:2

But Jesus knew that their strict insistence on the rituals prevented men from actually obeying God's commands:

> And why do you yourselves transgress the commandment of God for the sake of your tradition?
> —Matthew 15:3

Practicing traditions in nonflexible ways has led people throughout the history of Christianity to equate the traditions with God's commandments and teach them as such:

> "But in vain do they worship Me, teaching as doctrines the precepts of men." Neglecting the commandment of God, you hold to the tradition of men.
> —Mark 7:7, 8

Lest we think we are immune from the faults of the Pharisees, let us do a bit of self-examining. How do we evaluate the purity of a person's Christianity? Do we look at how well he maintains the rituals? Do we begin to think that anyone who does things differently than we do is heretical or non-Biblical? Do we judge people by whether they attend on Sunday nights? Do we raise our eyebrows if someone raises his hands during prayer or says an "Amen" out loud? Is it "unclean" to clap after special music or a sermon? Are drums "taboo" in the worship service? Is the reading of one particular version of the Bible "clean" while another is "impure"? Do we think that association with a person of another denomination will contaminate us?

Yes, it is possible to fall into the trap of judging a person's purity or impurity by the way we have always thought or done. It is not easy to look for inner purity, but Jesus said we must.

> Do not judge according to appearance, but judge with righteous judgment.
> —John 7:24

He was responding to those who were criticizing Him for being nontraditional. A person can be nontraditional and be right. Jesus proved that.

It is the inner character that determines our thoughts and attitudes:

> Not what enters into the mouth defiles the man, but what proceeds out of the mouth, this defiles the man . . . But the things that proceed out of the mouth come from the heart, and those defile the man.
> —Matthew 15:11, 18

It is possible to look clean on the outside, but be filthy on the inside:

> Woe to you, scribes and Pharisees, hypocrites! For you clean the outside of the cup and of the dish, but inside they are full of robbery and self-indulgence. You blind Pharisee, first clean the inside of the cup and of the dish, so that the outside of it may become clean also.
> —Matthew 23:25, 26

We must be extremely careful that we do not allow the righteousness we pursue (Matthew 5:6) or the mercy we extend to others (5:7) to become external only. We must keep our inner motives on target. We must extend mercy because we really appreciate God's mercy to us, and because we really care about people in need. God wants our inner characters to coincide with our outward actions. The Pharisees were concerned about clean hands, but God is concerned about clean hearts. The Pharisees were concerned about *ritual* purity, but God is concerned about *real* purity.

Becoming Pure

We initially become pure in heart because of the forgiveness offered by Jesus (Hebrews 9:14). *And we receive it by our faith (Acts 15:9).* Jesus was the initial provision for the purification of our hearts, and the Scriptures can continue to purify us (John 15:3). God also uses various kinds of situations to help keep us pure:

> In this greatly rejoice, even though now for a little while, if necessary, you have been distressed

by various trials, that the proof of your faith, being more precious than gold which is perishable, even though tested by fire, may be found to result in praise and glory and honor at the revelation of Jesus Christ.
—1 Peter 1:6, 7

As fire is used to burn foreign matter away from precious metals so that the pure stuff remains, so God allows various situations in order to show us what is hindering us from being Christlike:

The refining pot is for silver and the furnace for gold, but the Lord tests hearts.
—Proverbs 17:3

To maintain purity, though, we cannot only depend on God's action toward us; we must also act. We are commanded to flee and to pursue:

Now flee from your youthful lusts, and pursue righteousness, faith, love and peace, with those who call on the Lord from a pure heart.
—2 Timothy 2:22

One of the primary ways to remain pure in heart is to keep the goal in front of us. The objective we shoot for in the future affects our behavior in the present.

For instance, a young lady will make many plans and alterations in her schedule when she has a wedding in sight. Keeping that in view gets her through a lot of frustrations. In the same way, a student will go through many years of college with all the tension and toil involved as long as his goal is definite and in view.

If we lose sight of our goal, our motivation to

reach it will give out. If the goal is forgotten, we will become dropouts. John made it clear that the goal of Christlikeness will help people purify themselves in the present time:

> Beloved, now we are children of God, and it has not appeared as yet what we shall be. We know that, if He should appear, we shall be like Him, because we shall see Him just as He is. And everyone who has this hope fixed on Him purifies himself, just as He is pure.
> —1 John 3:2, 3

So, if we really want to be like Jesus, then we will be striving toward that goal constantly. But if we don't have that goal, we will not be trying to live like Him—we will not be pure in heart.

The Goal

Jesus said the "pure in heart" were to be congratulated and would be buoyant no matter what the difficulties, because they would "see God" (Matthew 5:8). This was not a new promise; it has always been a promise for those who remain pure. See Psalm 24:3-6.

The "pure in heart" can see God *now* if their eyes are open to see Him. God is not just in Heaven; He is also here. We serve a living and a present God. We can see Him in hands of mercy and in voices of cheer. We can see Him in the discipline that corrects us and the discourses (the Word) that guide us. We can see Him in the church—the dwelling place of God (Ephesians 1:22, 23; 2:22).

But if our hearts are not pure, we will not see Him now. Polluted hearts do not see what there is to see, for their vision is distorted. They see bad in everything:

> To the pure, all things are pure; but to those who are defiled and unbelieving, nothing is pure, but both their mind and their conscience are defiled.
>
> —Titus 1:15

The person who is always faultfinding has a "heart" problem. If he can't see God now because of his critical, belittling, carping, disparaging, and fussy disposition, he won't be able to see God later. He will need to undergo a heart purification first.

The "pure in heart" will see God when Jesus returns on Judgment Day. And they will become like Him on that day in all His perfectness. They will love Him, serve Him, and fellowship with Him forever. Those who have been washed in the "blood of the Lamb" (Revelation 7:14), and those whose purity is symbolized by their pure white linen, will reap the eternal blessings:

> "Let us rejoice and be glad and give the glory to Him, for the marriage of the Lamb has come and His bride has made herself ready." And it was given to her to clothe herself in fine linen, bright and clean; for the fine linen is the righteous acts of the saints.
>
> —Revelation 19:7, 8

They will reign forever with God where there will be no tears or pain, where only God's light will illumine the universe (21:4; 22:3-5).

The "pure in heart" will see God. That is a promise. Come quickly, Lord Jesus (Revelation 22:20).

Check Your Character*

                                                    Yes   No

1. Do you hope people will take
   notice of your accomplishments?
2. Would it bother you if you were
   counted absent from a service
   which you attended?
3. Does it bother you if your name
   is left off a list of people who
   contributed to a certain project?
4. When you give a large gift to the
   church, do you expect them to
   mount a plaque with your family
   name on it?
5. Do you think certain people
   receive too much attention in
   the church?
6. Do you pretend you are happy
   when you are not?
7. Do you have any secret sins?
8. Do you ever pretend to be friends
   with someone you don't like?
9. Do you tend to evaluate people by
   their church attendance only?
10. Do you ever give gifts anonymously?
11. Do you give money to the offering
    primarily because you know the good
    it will do others?
12. Are you on the inside what people
    see you to be on the outside?

*The "pure in heart" will answer "No" to the first
nine questions and "Yes" to the last three.

Chapter 9

Pursuing Peace

"Blessed are the peacemakers, for they shall be
called sons of God."

—Matthew 5:9

Someone has said that everybody loves a good fight. But I know Someone who doesn't. God does not enjoy those who break the peace. However, He does encourage, bless, and appreciate those who make peace.

If we live out the Beatitudes we have studied thus far, we will enjoy a lifestyle of God's peace; but if we do the opposite, our life will be filled with wars, factions, and everything that is opposed to peace.

The following chart illustrates the point:

Life of Peace	Life of Disruption
Humility (5:3)	Arrogance
+	+
Concern for Sin (5:4)	Disregard Sin
+	+
Self-control (5:5)	Lack of Self-control
+	+
Righteous Relation-ships (5:6)	Destroyed Relation-ships
+	+
Full of Mercy (5:7)	Full of Scorn
+	+
Pure Heart (5:8)	Polluted Heart
=	=
Peacemakers	Peacebreakers

The Meaning of Peace

A person can certainly not be a peacemaker unless he himself has peace. The word "peace" *(eirene)* means the absence of being molested in any way (Luke 11:21), the absence of confusion (1 Corinthians 14:33), the absence of disharmony (Luke 14:32), the absence of health and worry problems (Mark 5:34), and the absence of being despised (1 Corinthians 16:11). The Greek word was used to describe a person's calm thinking and friendly attitude.

Peace, however, does not just describe the absence of disharmony or people living in one accord. It has a much broader concept. It is what is needed for a person's total well-being—it is what makes a person *whole*. It describes a person who "has it all together," as in the popular venacular.

Peace as the world sees it and peace as God sees it are two different ideas. If we are not in a "shoot-'em-up" war, the world thinks we are at peace. But that type of peace is only superficial. Nations can be in a holding pattern and still not be at peace. Nations can call a "cease-fire" and give up the shooting because they are both worn out, but that may not be peace—especially if the people of the nations still think ill of one another, are suspicious of one another, and refuse to fellowship with one another.

Two individuals can declare a "truce," but never enter into a reconciled relationship. If the "truce" is not accompanied by good will and the desire for the well-being of the other, then peace has not yet come—even if the weapons (the fists or the tongue) have been put aside. How often the men of the world cry "Peace, peace" when there is no peace!

In contrast, it is possible for two individuals to argue occasionally but still be living in peace with one another. People can live in the middle of a war zone and still have peace within. Christians can be in the arena of persecution but still live in peace. Jesus was in peace as the nails were being pounded in His hands on the cross.

Peace was lost when man severed His relationship with God through sin, through disobedience. And as long as man and God's relationship is strained, man's relationship with himself and others will not be peaceful.

The war to end all wars did not end in 1918, but the war between God and man ended when Jesus rose from the grave. He died and rose again to dissolve the enemy relationship between God and man, and to restore the Father-child relationship. He also died and rose again to dissolve the enemy relationships that existed between men with one another and to bring them together into the same family, in which all the members live for the well-being of every other member (Ephesians 2:11-22). He came to crush the barriers that kept men at a distance from God and from each other. Through Jesus the many can become the one (Galatians 3:28).

Outside of Jesus, there is no peace on earth:

> For He Himself is our peace, who made both groups into one, and broke down the barrier of the dividing wall, by abolishing in His flesh the

> enmity, which is the Law of commandments
> contained in ordinances, that in Himself He
> might make the two into one new man, thus es-
> tablishing peace, and might reconcile them
> both in one body to God through the cross, by it
> having put to death the enmity.
> —Ephesians 2:14-16

The good news that we have for the world is that
the war that started in Genesis 3 can end for
each individual. No wonder it is called the "gospel of peace" (Ephesians 6:15). Peace is not the
result of the use of man's guns, but rather the
result of the extension of God's grace. We have
peace within when the Prince of Peace is within
us.

Making Peace

We must note that Jesus did *not* say in this
Beatitude—Blessed are the peace-*thinkers*, the
peace-*lovers*, or the peace-*talkers*. He said the
peace-*makers* were blessed. To be a child of God
we must be accomplishing peace; we don't just
accidently drift into it. We can't just be neutral
and passive and expect peace to come to us.

Right Conduct

Of course, the most significant way we can
make peace is to introduce the Prince of Peace
to people, to motivate people to reach out to
God—the God of peace—through evangelism.

This evangelism is not just a *talking* about
God, Jesus, and peace. It is also a *living out* in
our lives what peace means. Peace includes a
privilege (what God has given to us) and a *purpose* (what God expects from us). Jesus did not

93

come just to change our beliefs, but He came also to change our behavior.

We are commanded to live out the peace that is within us. We are told to actively *pursue* peace (2 Timothy 2:22). The word "pursue" *(diako)* means to run after, to chase down, to seriously and zealously track down. It means to stay in such hot pursuit that you never let it get away from you. The result is that you "get attached to" whatever you are chasing.

Yes, God gave us peace and calls us to peace (Colossians 3:15), but He also gave us a strong imperative to "preserve the unity of the Spirit in the bond of peace" (Ephesians 4:3).

But how do we pursue and maintain that peace that binds us together in unity? Paul tells us in Ephesians. In chapters 1-3, he tells us of the peace we have in Jesus; in chapters 4-6, he tells us how to maintain it: (1) We maintain the belief in one God (4:4-6), (2) We use our abilities for the well-being of others (4:7-16), (3) We set aside a life of hardness of heart and selfishness (4:17-24), (4) We practice integrity (4:25), (5) We don't let the sun go down on our anger (4:26), (6) We resist the devil (4:27), (7) We help people in need (4:28), (8) We use our tongues for the good of others (4:29), (9) We allow the Holy Spirit to work within us (4:30), (10) We put away bitter attitudes (4:31), (11) We practice sweet attitudes (4:32), (12) We imitate God (5:1), (13) We walk in love (5:2), (14) We live morally (5:3-18), (15) We have helpful fellowship with others (5:19, 20), (16) We have right relationships in our homes (5:21—6:4), (17) We respect the persons at work (6:5-9), and (18) We bring others to the Prince of Peace (6:10-20).

As we can readily see, making peace is not being passive. We are not to be like Rip Van Winkle who slept through life. He rocked no boats and created no waves. How peaceful—we might think. But that is not the peace of God.

God many times churns things up before the calmness comes. We remember that Jesus said, "Peace I leave with you" (John 14:27); but He also said, "Do not think that I came to bring peace on the earth; I did not come to bring peace, but a sword" (Matthew 10:34).

Was Jesus being inconsistent? If not, then how are these two ideas related? We have already seen how Jesus brings peace. But how does He bring a sword? The verse in Matthew 10 is within the context of Jesus' sending out the apostles to speak to families about deciding for or against Jesus. Any time a person decides to unite with Jesus, he must at the same time decide to disunite from the lifestyle that he had before—the lifestyle that is opposed to Christ. If he has been a member of another religious group (anti-Christ), he will be cut away from that religion with the sword of Jesus. That action often causes his relatives and/or friends to cut him off from their lives. For instance, parents may disown a child who converts to Jesus' lifestyle. A man's worst enemies might be the members of his own earthly family, because he has left the family traditions in order to become a part of the family of God. If a person is not willing to suffer that kind of severing relationship in order to be cemented to Jesus, then he is not worthy of Jesus who voluntarily became separated from His heavenly Father so we could be united with Him. Jesus has never asked us to do what He himself was not willing to do.

Jesus also brings a "sword" when He enlists us in a cosmic battle against Satan and His forces. However, that battle is not to be fought with guns and blades; but with truth, righteousness, peace, faith, salvation, the Word of God, and obedience (Ephesians 6:10-17; 2 Corinthians 10:3-6). We are to fight the good fight of faith (1 Timothy 1:18; 2 Timothy 4:7). But we are not to retaliate against evil with evil, but with good. Neither are we to take our own revenge, but we are to wait for God's revenge (Romans 12:17-21).

Of course, this is where the difficulty comes in. It is hard not to fight fire with fire. We must remember that we have more power than any laser beam. We have the eternal flame of the Holy Spirit which cannot be quenched by any human power. Our Commander-in-Chief is the *Almighty* One. If we pour into our skirmishes the tactics of the world, we will reap the world's results; if we do it God's way, we will reap eternal life (Galatians 6:7-9).

Right Attitudes

Before we can make peace in the ways mentioned, we must have an attitude overhaul. If our attitudes are strife causing, we cannot hope to be called peacemakers.

A "hot-tempered man" spreads strife (Proverbs 15:18). Could you be described in that way? Does your anger get away from your control?

"For lack of wood the fire goes out, and where there is no whisper, contention quiets down" (Proverbs 26:20). Do you keep the flames burning between certain individuals? Do you keep the topic of contention always before the group? I know of a youth minister who kept two groups of people burning with animosity toward one another. He kept running back and forth between the groups telling them what the others said, often taking the remarks out of context. He was causing a very deep rift in the relationships of those people. He was a peacebreaker, not a peacemaker.

The tragedy is compounded because it is so difficult to put the pieces together again after the relationship is broken. It is like trying to put Humpty-Dumpty together again; it is almost impossible. Anybody can break the peace and unity of a group of people, if we let him.

The one who breaks the peace is a fool: "The beginning of strife is like letting out water" (Proverbs 17:14a). Imagine the foolishness of standing in front of a dam and punching holes in it! After a little water starts trickling out, he starts thinking, "Wow! look what I have done!" He continues to pick the hole larger. How shocked the fool will be when he drowns in the flood of his own making! That is why the advice is to back off: "So abandon the quarrel before it breaks out" (17:14b).

A person who is constantly meddling in other's affairs is mentioned in this proverb: "Like one who takes a dog by the ears is he who passes by and meddles with strife not belonging to him" (26:17). How often would you walk up to a German Shepherd dog and start pulling his ears? It would be rather stupid, wouldn't it? It is just as stupid to barge into others' strife. You will be promoting peace if you stay out of what does not concern you.

Sometimes peace is made when we are willing to abandon our positions or opinions. We all need to learn how to yield in certain areas for the good of a relationship. I am thinking particularly of the marriage relationship. No marriage can be peaceful in God's way unless the husband and wife learn to yield to one another.

What if the husband wants to watch the football game on television, but the wife wants to watch a movie? For peace to prevail, someone has to yield. What if the husband wants to go on a wilderness camping trip for their vacation, but the wife wants to go to the beach? For peace to be present, someone must yield. What if the husband has no intention of taking out the garbage, but the wife thinks it is part of a man's job? For peace to prevade, someone must yield. Of course, I can hear many husbands saying, "Oh, yes, the wife must yield." No, fellas, it is a two-way yielding if it is Scriptural (Ephesians 5:21-29).

My wife is bothered greatly by the heat of summer. I am not. I'm concerned that we don't use much electricity, so the running of the air conditioner really bothers me. But I yield to my wife to promote her well-being. I don't want her to get a headache or become fatigued and irritable because of the heat. I allow her to turn on the air conditioner whenever she wishes.

My wife is good at math and bookkeeping. She could handle the finances for our family quite well, and she knows it. But I feel it is the duty of the head of the household to take care of this responsibility. Thus my wife yields to me for my well-being, to promote my self-image, and to let me know that she trusts me. For these and many other reasons, peace reigns at our house. Does it reign at yours? If not, are you yielding enough?

Of course, I am not saying that we must yield or compromise at every level of life to maintain peace. In matters relating to our eternal salvation, we must not yield. Remember, peace refers to whatever is for the well-being of another. (See Ecclesiastes 10:4.)

We also must watch our attitudes toward people of denominations. Do we look at them as enemies that we must defeat? Peace is found in Jesus, not in all of our understandings about all His words and teachings. Acting with animosity toward those who accept Christ as God's Son is anti-Christian, anti-Scriptural, and anti-natural. Anyone who is *in Christ* is our brother and our sister, and we ought to treat them as such.

He certainly did not intend for the followers of *His* day to be at "peace with one another" (Mark 9:50), while the disciples of *our* day are at war with one another. When we do so, we are scorning what He intended to accomplish through the cross. Let us not undo in a moment what God has planned to do through the centuries.

The Results

Some people will have quite a rude awakening when they realize that their doctrinal purity will not guarantee God's counting them as His children. Their pugnacious attitudes and conduct demolished their chances of being part of God's family. God is as interested in the living of our lives as He is in our theology. He will not consider us His children if cold hearts live next to correct heads.

God takes seriously the way we treat the others in His family. If you cannot live peaceably with another of God's children here on earth, then how will you get along with them in Heaven? Only peacemakers will be called the sons of God. Only those who imitate God will be called His children.

Jesus stressed this point later on in His Sermon on the Mount:

> You have heard that it was said, "You shall love your neighbor, and hate you enemy." But I say to you, love your enemies, and pray for those who persecute you in order that you may be *sons* of your Father who is in heaven.
> —Matthew 5:43-45

It is not easy to be a peacemaker, but we are equipped to do so. The Divine peacemaker lives within us and calls us to let His peace rule in our hearts (Colossians 3:15). (See Numbers 6:24-26 and 2 Corinthians 13:11.)

Congratulations to you who make peace, for you will live buoyantly and will be called a child of God!

Check Your Character*

Yes   No

1. Have you found your peace with God?
2. Do you express your regret to people when you think you might have hurt them?
3. Do you take the initiative to patch up tensions and problems?
4. Do you go directly to the people with whom you have a disagreement to try to iron out the difficulty?
5. Do you yield when you think your opinion on a nonessential matter may cause friction?
6. Do you think there are any other Christians outside of your "group"?
7. Do you enjoy an argument or a fight?
8. Do you know of someone with whom you do not have peace?
9. Do you "fly off the handle" often?
10. Do you ever gossip?
11. Do you ever go to bed angry?

*The peacemaker will answer "Yes" to the first six questions and "No" to the last five.

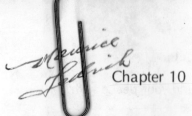

Chapter 10

Seeing Both Sides

"Blessed are those who have been persecuted for the sake of righteousness, for theirs is the kingdom of heaven. Blessed are you when men revile you, and persecute you, and say all kinds of evil against you falsely, on account of Me. Rejoice, and be glad, for your reward in heaven is great, for so they persecuted the prophets who were before you."

—Matthew 5:10-12

I really appreciate God's honesty. He wants us to become His children. He wants our thoughts, attitudes, and actions to mirror His—but He also wants us to know what we are getting into. He wants us to know what is on the other side of the mirror.

God tells us about the *blessings* and the *blastings* that will be in store for us if we follow His way. He tells us about the *gifts* and the *demands* of His kind of lifestyle. He tells us about the *rewards* and the *responsibilities* of being His children. He tells us about the *sweet* and the *bitter* side of life in Christ.

He wants us to come into Christianity with our eyes wide open to all the consequences. He fully intends for us to count the cost of discipleship as well as the dividends. The Gospel of Luke tells us this:

> Whoever does not carry his own cross and come
> after Me cannot be My disciple. For which one
> of you, when he wants to build a tower, does not
> first sit down and calculate the cost, to see if he
> has enough to complete it?
> —Luke 14:27, 28

Jesus makes clear to us in the Beatitudes that happiness and buoyancy come to us in the framework of persecution. He declared that we can expect persecution. He declared that we can expect persecution rather than praise, cruel insults rather than cordial invitations, reviling rather than respect, harassment rather than honor, abuse rather than applause, complaints rather than compliments, and slander rather than support.

The Forms

Persecution comes in many different packages. It may include physical violence, economical boycotts, social isolation, or verbal attacks. All of these have been experienced by God's children in the past and will continue to be until Jesus comes again.

During the early years of Christianity, Christians were imprisoned simply because of their faith. Some who had businesses were boycotted by all non-Christians, causing economical hardship. Sometimes their property was seized, and they were forced to flee to some other land (Hebrews 10:32-34).

Later, when the Christians would not admit that Caesar was god, they were rounded up, dipped in tar, fastened to poles, and placed around the edges of the athletic arenas. Their burning bodies served as illumination for the spectators to watch the sports events. And, of course, one of the favorite sports events was watching hungry animals devour Christians. The Christians would be wrapped in fresh animal skins and sent into the middle of the arena. Animals that had been purposely starved were then released to destroy the Christians in full view of the spectators.

Yes, at times throughout history it was physically dangerous to be a Christian. In some parts of the world this is still true.

Persecution through verbal attacks is also devastating. Harsh and bitter words can affect a person's physical health as well as his spiritual attitude (Proverbs 12:18; 15:4; 17:22; and 18:21). Words can cut very deeply and leave unhealed wounds. With their insidious damage (Proverbs 18:8), words can cause us to want to give up on our commitment. We wonder if it is worth it to have to undergo such abuse.

We can know, however, that if the words are false, and if they are said because we are standing up for Jesus, we will be blessed and rewarded (Matthew 5:11, 12). But if we are attacked because we are standing up for ourselves or our own opinions, that is an entirely different matter.

Persecution From Without

Any time two opposites live in the same vicinity conflict will emerge. Put a cat in the cage with a bird and watch the feathers fly! Put a dog and a skunk in a box together and —well, you know what would happen.

When you put people who have opposite value systems, opposite priorities, opposite lifestyles, and opposite goals in the same area, there will undoubtedly be conflict. One group will actually try to eliminate the presence or at least the influence of the other group (i.e., the white man and the Indians, the farmers and the cattlemen, the rich and the poor, etc.).

Many times there is open and violent conflict. At times compromises are reached. And as time goes on, some kind of assimilation takes place (which is the sly way to get rid of the opposition). Both groups start absorbing each others' values, methods, and goals. Their children and their cultures become intermarried. It becomes difficult to tell one group from another.

The Christian is different from those in the world—his values, priorities, goals, etc., are different from the world's. Because of that difference, he is persecuted. When Christians lose their uniqueness, when they become so absorbed in the world that an observer cannot tell the difference between them and non-Christians, the persecution will cease.

The true child of God who lives out the qualities of the Beatitudes will obviously not be sitting on the fence between Christianity and worldliness. He will stand firm and true on God's side. He will stick out "like a sore thumb" in the worldly culture, for his lifestyle and culture will be entirely different from the world's. Thus conflict will result, for the non-Christian way is hostile and conflicts with God's way (Romans 8:7).

A group of Christians are like a colony of Heaven on earth. They are citizens of a heavenly kingdom, which is not understood or liked by the world—thus the world resists its influence.

Some people, however, take Jesus' Beatitudes to mean that persecution is something we should desire and pursue. They think if we are not being persecuted that we must go out and seek it. At no time did Jesus say, "Blessed are the ones who *ask* for persecution," or "Blessed are the ones who *invite* persecution."

We are not persecuted because we request it, but because of righteousness' sake. If we are arrogant, act "holier than thou," impatient, opinionated, pushy, inconsiderate, and demanding our "rights," any type of attack on us would not be because of our righteousness. It would be because we are forcing ourselves on others. We would be inviting bad publicity because of our unrighteous attitudes.

How many times have you heard of a church in a negative way because the Christians in the church could not get along? I heard about a congregation that was redecorating the church building. The members could not agree on what color to paint the preacher's study. One group wanted to paint it blue; the other wanted to paint it a light pink. They argued about it for weeks. Finally the "blues" met in the middle of the week and painted the study blue. When the "pinks" saw the study on Sunday, they were quite incensed. So during that week they painted over the blue paint with pink paint. The paint store's sales increased considerably because the back and forth painting went on for several weeks. In the end the congregation split because of the difference of opinion over the color of paint.

That congregation got insults hurled at it for years by that community, but it was not because of righteousness. This tragedy resulted because the world got into the church more than the church got into the world.

Persecution From Within

Paradoxically, Christians will also receive persecution from those within the church. The first murder on earth was over a religious matter and a conflict within the same family (Genesis 4). Joseph was sold into slavery by his own brothers. David's life was threatened by King Saul, who had once loved and honored David. The prophets were stoned and imprisoned by God's people. Jesus' chief opponents were the religious leaders of Judaism. The apostles were opposed by the religious leaders (Acts 3—5). Stephen was killed by the religious Jews (Acts 7). Paul's chief hindrance to his preaching were the Jews of the synagogues. The Corinthians were beset by internal problems—Christian against Christian.

This type of persecution happens when someone challenges or threatens cherished traditions. When someone's opinion does not coincide with another's, often the lines are drawn and the battle commences. The trouble is very seldom caused because of the truths of God, but because of the doctrines and traditions of men which are treated as if they were from God.

107

Much of the persecution that we might receive from those within the church is done in all sincerity. Those who persecute you will think they are doing God a service.

The leaders in Jesus' day thought they were sticking by the Law in killing Him: "We have a law, and by that law He ought to die" (John 19:7). Jesus promised that His followers would be persecuted with that same kind of logic (John 16:2). Paul persecuted Christians because he was zealous for God (Acts 22:3; 26:9).

When the persecution from within the church comes upon us, let us be sure it is because of our righteousness. If it is, then we must not change our beliefs just to be accepted by the group. The Pharisees were only concerned about what the religious kinfolk would think of them. They were only concerned about being praised for their goodness (Matthew 6:1-6). Seeking praise can dilute our contribution to both God's kingdom and to the world around us. Praise can be dangerous. It can begin to control us; so much so, that we live mainly to receive it.

Those who will be persecuted in the church will be those in the congregation who are serving actively. Service makes people vulnerable because they are visible. The person who is doing little or nothing does not have to fear being persecuted. But the more a Christian works for God, the more of a chance he has of becoming the "turkey" at the religious turkey shoot.

When the disciples talked about greatness, Jesus channeled their thoughts in two directions: (1) greatness means service, (2) and greatness in service will invite opposition (Matthew 20:20-28). He said if they wanted to be great, they would have to be servants and be willing to drink of the cup that He drinks from (20:22, 23).

Those who are persecuted are not only the doers, but they are also the ones who speak up for the Lord. Jesus would not have been crucified if He had shut up. Instead He stirred up the people with His teaching (Luke 23:5).

Peter and John did not get into trouble with the religious leaders just by healing the cripple. It was the sermon that was preached that brought the opposition to a head (Acts 3). They were not ordered to quit doing good deeds; they were ordered not to speak in Jesus' name again (Acts 4:17, 18; 5:40).

I often hear this deceptive statement repeated: "Christian witnessing is best done by what we do, not by what we say." That is the coward's way out! If we don't speak up, people will never know *why* we do what we do. We have a message to share, not just services to perform.

Our Response

How should we respond when we are physically or verbally persecuted? First of all, we can leave. Jesus knew when to get out of a "hot spot" (Matthew 12:14, 15). Paul knew when to move on (Acts 13—20).

We must not compromise (Galatians 6:12; Acts 4:19, 20). We must continue doing what God commands even when ordered by men to stop (Acts 5:28, 29, 40-42). Whatever the consequences of the persecution, we must take them without retaliation (Romans 12:19; 1 Thessalonians 5:15).

Instead of being negative, we must be positive. We must seek to do good to our enemies (Romans 12:20, 21). We should pray for them by name, say good things about them, and verbally bless them while they blast us (Matthew 5:44-48). We must also forgive them publicly and privately (Acts 7:60).

We must stick to a life of godliness and use every opportunity to explain why we follow God's way (1 Corinthians 4:12, 13). If we do this, our persecutors will have no truthful reason for hurting us; they will have no grounds for their remarks or actions.

Our Reward

It is not easy to stand up and face persecution. But we can, if we keep our reward always within our view. The kingdom of Heaven is ours if we endure. "We are strangers here, waiting patiently to go where we belong."

Many in the world think they can gain kingdoms by using force, violence, and persecution. But God is the King of all kings and sits on the eternal throne of the universe. No one can replace Him, and His kingdom will always remain to be enjoyed by those who remain faithful to Him. We gain our kingdom by simply enduring and living in God's lifestyle. We gain the inheritance of the whole universe by developing godly characteristics and remaining in them no matter what the external circumstances might be.

We must also remember that our present troubles are only temporary (2 Corinthians 4:17, 18) and do not even come close to the degree of eternal blessing we will receive (Hebrews 11:13, 24-26).

Check Your Character*

		Yes	**No**

1. Have you counted the cost of living God's way?
2. Do the people at work know you are a Christian?
3. Has anyone asked you why you are so different?
4. Have you been ridiculed for your beliefs?
5. Do you pray for your enemies by name?
6. Do you ever help them out?
7. Have you forgiven your enemies?
8. Are you antagonistic about pushing your opinions in the church?
9. Do you verbally backbite fellow Christians who don't keep all the traditions the way you do?
10. Do you normally find fault with the morning sermon and say something about it to someone before lunch is over?

*The child of God who is persecuted for *righteousness* will answer "Yes" to the first seven questions and "No" to the last three.

Conclusion

Each of Jesus' Beatitudes include both privilege and purpose, both gift and demand. Each blessing He mentioned is a gift granted to us by our heavenly Father. We do not accomplish the blessings by ourselves or in ourselves, for the characteristics that result in the blessings are characteristics of God. In order to have those characteristics within us, we must have God's character living within us.

The privilege of having these characteristics and blessings in our lives is not all there is to it. Each characteristic is for the purpose of ministering to someone else. As we do, we are showing to others what God is like. Thus, we have the characteristics and blessings of God for the purpose of serving others. That is why Jesus said at the end of the Beatitudes, "Let your light shine before men in such a way that they may see your good works, and glorify your Father who is in heaven" (Matthew 5:16).

The light which is to shine out of our lives unto all men comes from the "bulb" (the source) of our godly characters. The world will not be able to know about or experience God's character unless they are exposed to it by God's children who mirror God's essence.

As we live out these qualities of life, we will be extremely visible; for each quality is opposed to the way the world acts and reacts. Jesus was making this point when He said, "You are the light of the world. A city set on a hill cannot be hidden" (Matthew 5:14).

If we have God's characteristics living within us, people will not have to go on a "search-and-find" mission to locate them. As light, we will be influential in canceling the darkness around us, giving people more illumination to see where they have been, where they are, and where they are heading with their lives. We may be the lighthouse that draws them to the eternal harbor of God's forgiving care. The characteristics inherent in the Beatitudes translate from attitudes within to activities without. And the force that emanates from that type of living is magnetic.

Jesus also said the qualities in the Beatitudes will provide salt in our lives: "You are the salt of the earth" (Matthew 5:13). Living in God's way with His character will cause the world to be thirsty, to want to drink from the eternal spring (John 4:14; 7:38, 39; Revelation 21:6). Our presence will cause people to desire God himself, to yearn to return to man's original likeness; for we were all created in God's likeness and will never be satisfied until we become aligned again with that image.

Besides making others thirsty, salt is also a preservative. The salt in our lives will serve to keep us from decaying and becoming rotten. As we live out God's character, we will be preserving the good that is in each of us. To withdraw this influence from our fellow Christians would be exposing them to the decaying influences of the world.

Of course, the best example of anyone living

out these Beatitudes is found in Jesus himself; for His mission was to demonstrate God's character to the world:

> No man has seen God at any time; the only begotten God, who is in the bosom of the Father, He has explained Him.
>
> —John 1:18

> Jesus said to him, "Have I been so long with you, and yet you have not come to know Me, Philip? He who has seen Me has seen the Father; how do you say, 'Show us the Father'?"
>
> —John 14:9

Jesus perfectly lived out the Beatitudes about which He spoke and in that way flawlessly displayed God to the world.

How was Jesus able to do that? The answer is two-fold: power and commitment. On the one hand He was conceived of the Holy Spirit (Matthew 1:20)—the power. On the other hand, He was determined to obey God (John 5:30; 12:49)—the commitment.

We cannot expect to live out these Beatitudes by any lesser means. We also need to be conceived by the Holy Spirit. We can do so by turning our lives over to Christ, by believing in Him, by repenting of doing things *our* way, and by turning to do things God's way. We can bury our old attitudes and behavior patterns in baptism, and at the same time put on Jesus (Galatians 3:27). We will then be raised with Him to walk in a new way of life (Romans 6:4).

> Therefore we have been buried with Him through baptism into death, in order that as Christ was raised from the dead through the

> glory of the Father, so we too might walk in new-
> ness of life.
>
> —Romans 6:4

The new life receives its power through the working of the indwelling presence of the Holy Spirit
(Acts 2:38).

> And Peter said to them, "Repent, and let each
> of you be baptized in the name of Jesus Christ
> for the forgiveness of your sins; and you shall
> receive the gift of the Holy Spirit."
>
> —Acts 2:38

"He saved us, not on the basis of deeds which
we have done in righteousness, but according to
His mercy, by the washing of regeneration and
renewing by the Holy Spirit" (Titus 3:5). When
we put on the new self, our minds will be renewed. "And that you be renewed in the spirit of
your mind, and put on the new self, which in the
likeness of God has been created in righteousness and holiness of the truth" (Ephesians 4:23,
24). It is as if we were born again and become
new creatures. "Therefore if any man is in
Christ, he is a new creature; the old things
passed away; behold, new things have come" (2
Corinthians 5:17).

Then, just as in our physical lives, growth begins right after birth. We must constantly seek to
grow into Jesus' likeness. "Speaking the truth in
love, we are to grow up in all aspects into Him,
who is the head, even Christ" (Ephesians 4:15).
This is a daily process. "Therefore we do not lose
heart, but though our outer man is decaying, yet
our inner man is being renewed day by day" (2

Corinthians 4:16). It involves commitment (1 Peter 2:2). Living as Christ lived will mean we will live out the characteristics of the Beatitudes.

Seeing the Beatitudes put into action is like seeing a mirrored reflection of Jesus in action on earth again:

> But we all, with unveiled face beholding as in a mirror the glory of the Lord, are being trans-formed into the same image from glory to glory, just as from the Lord, the Spirit.
> —2 Corinthians 3:18

And as we think of the Beatitudes, we should remember another one: "If you know these things, you are blessed if you do them" (John 13:17). These Beatitudes are not just to be memorized, studied, or meditated upon—they are for the doing. You are to be congratulated if you *do* them!